# UPPER MIDWEST GERMAN BIOGRAPHICAL INDEX

Don Heinrich Tolzmann

HERITAGE BOOKS
2013

**HERITAGE BOOKS**
***AN IMPRINT OF HERITAGE BOOKS, INC.***

**Books, CDs, and more—Worldwide**

For our listing of thousands of titles see our website
at
www.HeritageBooks.com

Published 2013 by
HERITAGE BOOKS, INC.
Publishing Division
5810 Ruatan Street
Berwyn Heights, Md. 20740



International Standard Book Numbers
Paperbound: 978-1-55613-884-3
Clothbound: 978-0-7884-6840-7

Table of Contents


| | |
|---|---|
| Preface | vii |
| Sources Indexed | ix |
| Index | 1 |
| A (Abbelen-Azarias) | 1 |
| B (Baas-Buxa) | 4 |
| C (Cahensley-Czudnochowski) | 17 |
| D (Dablon-Dysterheft) | 20 |
| E (Eberbach-Eyme) | 24 |
| F (Faber-Fusz) | 26 |
| G (Gackenheimer-Gwinnder) | 31 |
| H (Haack-Hyer) | 37 |
| I (Igenfritz-Iversen) | 48 |
| J (Jachinski-Jungmann) | 48 |
| K (Kaas-Kutrib) | 50 |
| L (LaBusch-Lyser) | 62 |
| M (Maas-Myer) | 66 |
| N (Nägele-Nusser) | 75 |
| O (Obenauer-Overrocker) | 77 |
| P (Pabst-Putthoff) | 79 |
| Q (Quant-Quinius) | 84 |
| R (Raab-Russer) | 84 |
| S (Sachs-Syke) | 90 |
| T (Tachick-Twachtman) | 110 |
| U (Ubert-Uthe) | 112 |
| V (Vail-Vrooman) | 113 |

W (Wachall-Wurster) 114

Y (Yahr-Yunck) 122

Z (Zabel-Zysk) 122

# Preface

The pupose of the Upper Midwest German Biographical Index (UMGBI) is to provide access to German-American historical sources which focus on the Upper Midwest. This includes coverage of several states, including Illinois, Iowa, Michigan, Minnesota, and Wisconsin. It complements the Ohio Valley German Biographical Index and its Supplement, which provide coverage of other Midwestern states. Altogether almost 6,000 names are indexed in the UMGBI.

This index is arranged alphabetically, and after each name a symbol will be found which refers to the work, or works, where that particular name is listed. The amount of information varies from extensive biographical articles, biographical notices, obituaries, to brief references. The UMGBI facilitates access to these sources, and provides biographical indexing on a geographical scale to the German element in the area which is nowhere else available. Non-German names in the sources, it should be noted, were excluded from this index.

The editor would here like to express a special word of gratitude to Mr. Thomas Winter, doctoral candidate in American history in the History Department of the University of Cincinnati, for his invaluable research assistance in the preparation of this index.

It is hoped that this work will be of assistance to all those who are interested in locating biographical references to German-Americans in the Upper Midwest.

Don Heinrich Tolzmann
University of Cincinnati

## Sources Indexed

(A) Anuta, Michael J. *East Prussians from Russia*. Menominee, Michigan: Anuta, 1979.

(E) Eiboeck, Joseph. *Die Deutschen von Iowa und deren Errungenschaften: Eine Geschichte des Staates, dessen deutscher Pioniere und ihrer Nachkommen*. Des Moines, Iowa: Druck und Verlag des Iowa Staatsanzeiger, 1900.

(F) Frank, Louis F. *Pionierjahre der deutsch-amerikanischen Familien Frank-Kerler in Wisconsin und Michigan, 1849-1864. Geschildert aus Briefen*. Milwaukee, 1911.

(G1) Glasrud, Clarence A., ed. *A Heritage Deferred: The German-Americans in Minnesota*. Moorhead, MN: Concordia College, 1984.

(G2) Glasrud, Clarence A., ed. *A Heritage Fulfilled: The German-Americans*. Moorhead, MN: Concordia College, 1984.

(GM) *Geschichte der Minnesota-Synode und ihrer einzelnen Gemeinden. Ein Gedenkstein zum Fuenfzigjaehrigen Synodal-Jubilaeum, 1860-1910*. St. Louis, MO: Druck und Verlag der Louis Lange Publishing Co., 1909.

(H) Hofmeister, Rudolf. *The Germans of Chicago*. Champaign, IL: Stipes Pub. Co., 1976.

(HJ) Hense-Jensen, Wilhelm. *Wisconsin's Deutsch-Amerikaner bis zum Schluss des neunzehnten Jahrhunderts*. Milwaukee: Im Verlage der Deutschen Gesellschaft; Druck der Germania, 1900.

(K) Koss, Rudolf H. *Milwaukee*. Milwaukee: Schnellpressen-Druck des Herold, 1871.

(R) Russell, John Andrew. *The Germanic Influence in the Making of Michigan*. Detroit: University of Detroit, 1927.

(S) Schneider, Carl E. *The German Church on the American Frontier. A Study in the Rise of Religion among the Germans of the West. Based on the History of the Evangelischer Kirchenverein des Westens* (Evangelical Church Society of the West, 1840-1866). St. Louis: Eden Pub. House, 1939.

(SH) Steinhauser, Frederic R. *New Ulm, Minnesota Germans: Adults of German Birth Settled in New Ulm and Surrounding Areas 1860*. n.p., n.d.

(T) Tolzmann, Don Heinrich, "Members of the German Musical Society of Milwaukee in 1900," *Journal of German-American Studies*, vol. 11, no. 2 (1976): 25-29.

(TC) Townsend, Andrew Jacke. *The Germans of Chicago.* Chicago: Deutsch-Amerikanische Historische Gesellschaft, 1932.

(W) Weiland, Evelyn, ed. *Of Pilgimage, Prayer and Promise: A Story of St. Mary's, Westphalia 1836-1986*. Westphalia, Michigan: Westphalia Historical Society, 1986.

Index


Abbelen, Peter (G1)

Abbott, -- (K)

Abbott, Chas. (K)

Abbott, Edith (H)

Abbott, Frederick H. (R)

Abe, W. (K)

Abel, F. (K)

Abel, Frank Lawrence (R)

Abel, Fritz (R)

Abel, John Jacob (R)

Abel, Julius Caesar (R)

Abel, Sylvester (R)

Abele, J. G. (S)

Abert, Georg (HJ, K)

Abert, James William (R)

Abert, Colonel John (R)

Abfalter, Francis (W)

Abner, Henry (TC)

Abrams, B. A. (T)

Abresch, Chas. (T)

Acker, M. (K)

Acker, Captain William H. (G2)

Ackeremann, Cecilia (W)

Ackermann, Frieda (H)

Ackermann, Prof. U. (GM)

Ackle, Stephen (R)

Adams, C. F. (H)

Adams, C. K. (HJ)

Adams, -- (HJ)

Adams, John (HJ)

Adams, John (SH)

Adamy, Peter H. (R)

Adelbert, Brother -- (R)

Adelmann, Gottfried (W)

Adendorf, John (R)

Adler, D. (T)

Adler, Dankmar (H)

Adler, David (HJ)

Adler, E. D. (T)

Adler, S. (K)

Affeld, Charles (H)

Affeld, Frank (H)

Affholtler, Franz Joseph (W)

Ahner, H. (H)

Ahrenweld, Frank A. (R)

Aigner, Dr. Gottfried (HJ, K)

Alber, Frederick (R)

Albert, Philipp J. (S)

Alberti, Alexander (R)

Albrecht, Albert A. (R)

Albrecht, Pastor C. J. (GM)

Albrecht, Ernest (G2)

Albrecht, Frederick (SH)

Albrecht, Pastor G. T. (GM)

Albrecht, Pastor Gottl. (GM)

Albrecht, Jakob (H)

Albrecht, Pastor Jm. F. (GM)

Albrecht, Pastor J. Ch. (GM)

Albrecht, Louise Hanna (SH)

Albrecht, Pastor W. C. (GM)

Albright, Dr. C. E. (T)

Albright, Egbert (R)

Alexander, J.H. (HJ)

Allen, Eben (R)

Allgeyer, Rev. Ferdinand (R)

Allis, E.B. (HJ)

Allmendinger, Daniel Frederick (R)

Allwardt, Rev. H.A. (HJ)

Almerian, Brother -- (R)

Alster, A. (K)

Alter, -- von (HJ)

Altgeld, John P. (H, TC)

Alton, Frederick (R)

Altpeter, Oscar (HJ)

Alwin, Wilheim (SH)

Alwin, Wilhelmina (SH)

Amberg, Adam (H)

Amberg, David M. (R)

Amberg, Franz (H)

Amberg, J. (K)

Ambruster, Jacob (R)

Ameis, Nicholas (R)

Amelung, Frederick (R)

Amend, Conrad (E)

Amian, Brother -- (R)

Ammeling, Pastor Gilbert (R)

Ammerman, -- (R)

Ammermann, Jos. (HJ)

Ammo, J. (HJ)

Amrhein, -- (R)

Amrhein, John (R)

Andersen, H. H. (E)

Anderson, John (HJ)

Anderson, Melville Best (R)

Anderson, Prof. R. B. (HJ)

Andre, Pater -- (HJ)

Andre, Gustavus (SH)

Andre, Josephine (SH)

Andres, Anton (W)

Andres, Paul Gerhard ()

Andries, Engelbert (R)

Andries, Henry A. (R)

Andrew, Brother -- (R)

Angell, James R. (R)

Angle, Paul (H)

Angler, William R. (R)

Ankele, David C. (S)

Anneke, Emil (R)

Anneke, Fritz (HJ, K)

Anneke, Henriette (K)

Anneke, Mathilde Franziska (HJ, K)

Annen, Mathias (W)

Annen, Peter (H)

Anschütz, Leo (HJ)

Ansted, Chr. (T)

Ansted, G. (HJ)

Anthon, George, Christian (R)

Antonius, Frederick W. (R)

Antrobus, John (R)

Anuta, Mary (A)

Anuta, Michael, Jr. (A)

Anuta, Michael, Sr. (A)

Anuta, Wilhelmina (A)

Anutta, Frederick (A)

Anutta, Frederick, Jr. (A)

Anutta, John Bedford (A)

Anutta, Martha (A)

Anutta, William (A)

Apel, Franz A. (R)

Appel, -- (HJ)

Appel, Charles (H)

Appel, Louis (H)

Arcularius, Eduard (S)

Arend, William (H)

Arends, Robert M. (R)

Arendt, Pastor F. W. M. (R)

Arendt, Francis (SH)

Arens, -- (HJ)

Arens, Henry (G1)

Arens, John (W)

Arns, John N. (R)

Arens, John Peter (W)

Arens, Wilhelm (H)

Arentz, U. S. S. (R)

Arets, -- (R)

Argus, John (R)

Armbruster, Wendelon (W)

Arnd, Hugo E. R. (R)

Arndt, A. H. (H)

Arndt, Albert F. R. (R)

Arndt, Christopher (R)

Arndt, Jacob (R)

Arndt, John P. (HJ)

Arnemann, Alfred (E)

Arnold, A. C. (T)

Arnold, F. (K)

Arnold, G. (E)

Arnold, J. (K)

Arnzten, Bernard (TC)

Arpfe, Jerome G. (HJ)

Arpfe, Geb. (HJ)

Asboth, Brigadier General -- (HJ)

Asche, Wilhelm (H)

Aschermann, A. F. (T)

Aschermann, Ed. (HJ)

Aschmann, W. (K)

Askin, John, Jr. (R)

Askin, John, Sr. (R)

Asman, John (R)

Asmuth, Anton (HJ, T)

Aste, Christian (H)

Astor, John Jacob (R)

Auch, Pastor John J. (R)

Auer, John (R)

Auer, Louis (HJ, K)

Augenstein, C. (H)

Aulenbach, Karl (S)

Auler, Dr. -- (K)

Aulmann, William (E)

Austmann, Ludwig (S)

Avers, H. F. (T)

Azarias, Brother -- (R)

Baas, -- (K)

Baasen, Francis (G1, K, SH)

Babler, Fridolin (HJ)

Babler, Oswald (HJ)

Babst, Earl F. (R)

Bach, Christoph (HJ, K)

Bach, Rudolf (H)

Bach, Samuel (S)

Bach, Wilhelm (HJ)

Bachelle, Werner von (HJ)

Bacher, -- (R)

Bachhofer, Ludwig (H)

Bachhuber, M. (K)

Backus, Frederick (R)

Bade, Alb. (K)

Bade, Henry, Sr. (R)

Badem, J. P. (H)

Bader, Bernhard (R)

Badin, J. B. (HJ)

Bading, Rev. John (HJ)

Badora, Maria (A)

Badura, August (A)

Badura, Charles (A)

Badura, Frederick (A)

Badura, Gottfried (A)

Badura, Maria (A)

Badura, Paul (A)

Baensch, Emil (HJ)

Baer, Christopher (R)

Baer, Joseph (SH)

Baer, Lorenz (H)

Baereke, Mar. (HJ)

Baetz, Henry (HJ, T)

Bahlke, Wm. A. (R)

Baier, Johann (H)

Baierlein, Emil (R)

Baker/Becker, John Peter (W)

Balatka, Hans (H, HJ, K, TC)

Balcke, Alphonse (R)

Balk, H. G. (HJ)

Ball, Joseph (G1)

Ballen, Frederick (R)

Baltzer, Adolph H. (S)

Band, Henry (H)

Bandholz, Harry H. (R)

Banga, Heinrich (H)

Bank, Henry (E)

Bank, Johann (S)

Bapiro, Wm. (HJ)

Baraga, Rt. Rev. Frederick (R)

Baraga, Friedrich (HJ)

Barath, Herman (R)

Barbier, Catharina (SH)

Barbier, Jacob (SH)

Barbour, Levi L. (R)

Barck, Eduard (F)

Bardeen, Charles Russell (R)

Barie, Wm. (R)

Barker, Frederick (W)

Barlage, Anton F. (R)

Barlow, Brigadier General -- (HJ)

Barnard, Harry (H)

Barnay, -- (HJ)

Barnetz, D. (R)

Barnhart, Peter (R)

Barnhart, Willard (R)

Barrager, John (R)

Barstow, Gouverneur -- (HJ)

Bartell, C. F. (HJ)

Bartelme, J. (HJ)

Bartels, J. L. (HJ)

Barth, Heinrich (R)

Barth, John (T)

Barth, Nicholas (H)

Barth, Otto (SH)

Barth, Peter (T)

Barth, Phillip (H)

Barth, Robert J. (T)

Barthel, Dr. G. (K)

Barthold, Richard (TC)

Bartz, Pastor A. C. (GM)

Barwig, Chas. (HJ)

Basse, G.D. (HJ)

Bast, Peter (W)

Bastian, -- (HJ)

Battermann, William (H)

Bauck, Paul (R)

Bauer, -- (K)

Bauer, Ad. (K)

Bauer, August (H)

Bauer, Edw. A. (T)

Bauer, Emil (R)

Bauer, John M. (H)

Bauer, Joseph (W)

Bauer, Julius (H)

Bauer, O. (K)

Bauer/Bour, Peter (W)

Bauer, Wm. (T)

Bauerlein, J. G. (R)

Baum, Christoph (H)

Baum, Georg (H)

Baum, Jesse (R)

Bauman, Rev. John A. (R)

Baumann, Edward (H)

Baumann, Franz (H)

Baumann, Pastor J. R. (GM)

Baumann, John F. (E)

Baumbach, Dr. -- (K)

Baumbach, Chas. v. (T)

Baumbach, Kurt (H)

Baumbach, L. von (HJ)

Baumbach, Ernst von (HJ)

Baumbach, Moritz von (HJ)

Baumgärtner, Pastor -- (K)

Baumgärtner, Henry (HJ)

Baumgaertner, Wilhelm (HJ)

Baumgarten, brothers (H)

Baumgarten, C. (T)

Baumgarten, Catherine (H)

Baumgarten, Charles (H)

Baumgarten, Franz (T)

Baumgarten, Moritz (TC)

Baumgarten, Otto C. (T)

Baumler, Caroline (SH)

Baumler, G. Edward (SH)

Baur, Bertha (R)

Baur, Pastor J. (GM, K)

Baur, John C. (R)

Baus, John (H)

Bauskey, Joseph (H)

Baxmann, Johann (H)

Beaber, Wm. (A)

Beachnau/Pitschnau, Fredrick (W)

Bearinger, J. L. (R)

Bechard, David (R)

Becher, F. A. (HJ)

Becher, J. A. (HJ, T)

Becherer, G. C. (T)

Bechtel, Pastor Phil. (GM)

Bechtele, Peter (E)

Bechtner, Paul (HJ)

Beck, brothers (H)

Beck, Adam (T)

Beck, C. A. (T)

Beck, Carl (H)

Beck, Christian (S)

Beck, George (SH)

Beck, Gottlieb (R)

Beck, Johan Heinrich (R)

Beck, Karl (HJ)

Beck, Theresia (SH)

Becker, Alvis (E)

Becker, C. F. (K)

Becker, Caspar (HJ)

Becker, Francis (R)

Becker, Fridolin (HJ)

Becker, Fritz (H)

Becker, Gustav (E)

Becker, Rev. J. (HJ)

Becker, J. A. (HJ)

Becker, Joseph (TC)

Becker, Jost (HJ)

Becker, Leopold (H)

Becker, Marie (HJ, K)

Becker, Matthias (R)

Becker, Melchior (R)

Becker, Theodore (R)

Becker, Wm. (HJ, T)

Becker, William (H)

Beckers, Oscar (H)

Beckman, -- (R)

Bedenbiender,/Biedenbender (W)

Bednarz, Caroline (A)

Bednarz, Frederick (A)

Bednarz, John G. (A)

Bednarz, Louise (A)

Bednarz, Martin (A)

Bednarz, Michael (A)

Bednarz, Mollie (A)

Bednarz, William (A)

Bedora, Minnie (A)

Bedora, Mollie (A)

Bedura, Michael (A)

Beebe, Georg (H)

Beem, Martin (H)

Beerhorst, Henry (R)

Behagel, Daniel

Behaim, Martin (G2)

Behaum, Martin (R)

Behlke, Henry (SH)

Behnke, Albert (SH)

Behnke, Bertha (SH)

Behnke, Frederick (SH)

Behnke, Sophia (SH)

Behr, Lorenz (R)

Behrans, Charles August (R)

Beicke, Jean (G2)

Beiderbecke, Bix (H)

Beiersdorf, Jacob (H)

Beil, Carl (H)

Beinder, H. (TC)

Beinhorn, Ferdinand (G2)

Beinhorn, Frederick (SH)

Beinhorn, Henry (SH)

Beinhorn, Joanna (SH)

Beinhorn, Maria (SH)

Beiniger, -- (K)

Beisel, Peter, Jr. (R)

Beissel, Charles (A)

Beissel, Charles (A)

Beissel, Henry (A)

Beissel, Konrad (G2)

Beissel, Louis (A)

Beiter, Nikolaus (E)

Belen/Behlen, Christopher (W)

Belitz, Henry (HJ)

Belke, Anton (W)

Belknap, Dr. -- (K)

Beller, Jacob (R)

Bellheimer, Joseph (R)

Bellm, John (SH)

Bellm, Rosa (SH)

Belser, Carl William (R)

Beltenbender, Heinrich (R)

Beltenbender, Peter (R)

Belz, John (H)

Belzer, -- (R)

Benada, Martin (H)

Bender, -- (K)

Bender, Georg (H)

Bendix, Max (R)

Benefeldt, Alfred (H)
Bener, Matt (H)
Bengel, Thomas (W)
Beninghoff, Frederick (R)
Benjamin, H. M. (T)
Benner, John (W)
Bennett, Michael (HJ)
Bennett, W. C. (HJ)
Benrodt, A. (K)
Benroth, Adolph (H)
Bent, Frederic (R)
Bentzen, Frederick Whelpley (R)
Benz, George (G2)
Benzel, Norbert (G2)
Benzenberg, G. H. (T)
Benzenberg, George Henry (R)
Berberich, Prof. Francis (R)
Berdell, Charles (H)
Berdell, Nicholas (H)
Berens, August (H)
Berens, Peter (H)
Berg, brothers (H)
Berg, Anton (TC)
Berg, Louis (H)
Bergemen, Louis (R)
Bergenthal, Aug. (T)
Bergenthal, Wm. (HJ, T)
Berger, Eduard (S)
Berger, Jacob (R)
Berger, Victor (HJ)
Berger, W. (K)
Berger, Wm. (T)
Berges, Dietrich (S)
Berghle, Ellmer (R)
Bergmann, Carl (H)
Bergmann, Henry C. (SH)
Bergmann, Maria C. (SH)
Bergrath, Theodore (W)
Bergsträsser, Arnold (H)
Beringer, Hedwig (HJ)
Berk, Conrad (E)
Berkey, Julius (R)
Berndt, Julius (SH)
Bernhard, Dr. A. (T)
Bernhard, Eduard (E)
Bernhardt, Martin (R)
Berniger, J. H. (K)
Bers, Abraham (R)
Bert, Edward (H)
Bertram, Agnes (H)
Bertram, Lorenz (W)
Bertsch, Catherine (A)

Bertsch, Christian (R)

Bertsch, Frederick (A)

Bertsch, Gottlieb (A)

Bertsch, Michael (A)

Bertschy, Frln. [Ms.] -- (K)

Bertschy, Jac. (K)

Bertschy, John (K)

Bertz, George B. (R)

Berwald, John (E)

Besle, -- (R)

Bessinger, Conrad (R)

Best, Anna (H)

Best, Carl (K)

Best, Chas. (T)

Best, Emil (T)

Best, Fred (T)

Best, Jacob (HJ, K, T)

Best, Lorenz (HJ, K)

Best, Mattias (H)

Best, Philipp (HJ, K)

Betterle, -- (R)

Bettinger, Melchior (R)

Bettmann, Bernhard (H)

Betz, Andreas (SH)

Betz, John (H)

Betz, Konrad (S)

Betzing, Christian (R)

Beverung, H. C. (K)

Beyer, B. A. (H)

Beyer, Christian (R)

Beyer, Fr. (K)

Bialy, Augusta (A)

Bickel, William (G2)

Bicklen, G. H. (E)

Bickler, Peter (HJ)

Bidtel, Dr. E. (T)

Bieber, Adam (A)

Bieber, Fred (A)

Bieber, Fred, Jr. (A)

Bieber, Fred, Sr. (A)

Bieber, Martha (A)

Bieber, Minnie (A)

Bieber, Paul (HJ)

Bieber (?), Pauline (A)

Biebrich, -- (K)

Biedermann, A. (H)

Biedermann, A. J. (HJ, K)

Biederstein, Frank (HJ)

Bielawski, -- (K)

Bielfeld, E. A. (T)

Bielfeld, H. G. (T)

Bielfeld, W. (K)

Bielefeld, A. H. (HJ)

Bielefeld, Frank (H)

Bieregans, Frederick (W)

Bielfeld, Heinrich A. (HJ)

Bierbaum, Harold (G2)

Biermann, Christian (H)

Biermann, Gustav (E)

Biersach, -- (K)

Biersach, Adolf (HJ)

Biersach, Aug. (K, T)

Biersach, Louis D. (T)

Biersach, M. (HJ)

Biersach, W. (K)

Biersach, Wm. (T)

Biesemeier, Wilhelm (S)

Bierstetel/Bierstettel, Franz Joseph (W)

Bigelow, F. G. (T)

Bigler, Philip (R)

Binder, Heinrich (H)

Binder, Karl (H)

Bingenheimer, P. (K)

Bink, John (H)

Binner, Wilhelm F. (S)

Binzel, Jacob (T)

Birkenwald, Samuel (HJ, T)

Birkhoff, George David (R)

Birkinstock, Adolph (R)

Birkner, Friedrich (S)

Bischoff, Catherine (R)

Bischof, Herman (R)

Bischoff, Herman (R)

Bishop, Frank Jr. (HJ)

Bishop/Bischoff, Joseph Alexander (W)

Bittenbender, -- (R)

Bittner, Walter Simon (R)

Black, John (T)

Blaeser, Anton (W)

Bland, -- (HJ)

Blatz, Barbara (HJ, K)

Blatz, Caspar (HJ)

Blatz, Valentin (HJ)

Blatz, Valentin, Jr. (HJ)

Blatz, Frau Val. (T)

Blauel, C. (K)

Blauert, Lehrer [teacher] (GM)

Blank, G.A. (H)

Blasen Johann (H)

Blasie, Bernhard (H)

Blatz, A. C. (T)

Blatz, Emil (T)

Blatz, Valentin (H, HJ)

Blatz, Val., Jr. (T)

Blecken, Carl H. (SH)

Blecken, Mary C. (SH)

Blein, Joseph (R)

Blenker, Brig. Gen. -- (HJ)

Blesch, August F. (R)

Bless, John (H)

Bletsch, Jacob (H)

Bleyer, Georg (HJ)

Bleyer, H. M. (HJ)

Bleyer, Heinrich (HJ)

Bleyer, Julius (HJ)

Bliesernicht, Prof. E. R. (GM)

Bliset, Peter (R)

Blitz, Louis (R)

Bloch, Konrad (H)

Block, Ernst (HJ)

Block, Herbert (H)

Blocki, Frederick (H)

Bloedel, A. (T)

Blohm, G. A. (E)

Bloomfield-Zeisler, Fanny (H)

Blüss, C. (H)

Blum, J. (K)

Blum, Elisabeth (SH)

Blum, Martin (SH)

Blumer, Pastor Adam (GM)

Blumenfeld, Mar. (HJ)

Blundy/Blonde,
Francis J., Sr. (W)

Bluthardt, Mrs. Theodor (H)

Bluthardt, Theodor (H)

Boas, Jacob (H)

Bochman, Christian (R)

Bochman, Poly (R)

Bock, Dr. -- (HJ)

Bock, Joseph Carl (R)

Bockharst, Rev. Aloysius (R)

Bodden, A. G. (T)

Bode, -- Jr. (K)

Bode, B. A. (K)

Bode, C. F. (K)

Bode, Kaspar H. (S)

Bode, Wm. F. (HJ)

Bodenbach, P. (K)

Bodenbach, Paul (T)

Bodenstab, Adolph (HJ)

Bodenstedt, Fried. (HJ)

Bodmer, Johann J. (S)

Boebel, Hans (HJ, K)

Boebel, Heinrich (HJ, K)

Boeckmann, W. C. (H)

Böhm, G. (K)

Boehm, George P. (TC)

Boelte, Christ. (HJ)

Boeppler, William (TC)

Boesche, Barbara (SH)

Boesche, Henry (SH)

Bösel, A. (HJ, K)

Boeppler, William (H, HJ)

Boehler, Chas. A. (E)

Boerner, John (H)

Börngen, H. (HJ)

Boeske, Heinrich (H)

Böttcher, Pastor -- (GM)

Boettcher, Dorothea (H)

Böttcher, Pastor H. (GM)

Böttner, Wilhelm (H, TC)

Bötzow, -- (HJ, K)

Bogard, Jacob (R)

Bogen, Ludwig (G2)

Bogling, Pastor Friedrich (R)

Bogt, W. (K)

Bohlen -- (HJ)

Bohling, William (R)

Bohn, G. F. (HJ)

Bohn, Dr. William F. (TC)

Bohlander, Rev. Geo. (E)

Bohr, Anna (W)

Bohr, Frank (R)

Bohr, Michael (W)

Bolander, Johann (H)

Bolander, Olga (A)

Bold, F. C. (H)

Boldenweck, William (H)

Bollman, Edward (R)

Bolter, Andreas (H)

Bolza, Charles (R)

Bomino, P. (H)

Bonduel, Florimond J. (HJ, K)

Boock, Frederick (SH)

Boock, John W. (GM)

Boock, Mary (SH)

Boos, E. (K)

Boos, F. (H)

Borchert, Albert (H)

Borchert, C. (T)

Borchert, Friedrich (HJ, K)

Borgman, Sylvia Irene (R)

Borick, William C. (R)

Borkowski, Frederick (A)

Borkowski, Gottlieb (A)

Borkowski, John (A)

Borkowski, Ludwig (A)

Borkowski, Gust (A)

Bormann, Christ (E)

Born, R. (K)

Borneman, Dedrich (R)

Borngesser, G. F. (K)

Bornman, John (R)

Borse, James R. (R)

Borutta, Gottlieb (A)

Borutta, William (A)

Borutta, Gottlieb (A)

Bosche, Rev. Aloysius F. (R)

Boskche, Julius (R)

Bossert, Gottlob (HJ, T)

Bott, Barbara (SH)

Bott, Peter (SH)

Bott, Valentin (SH)

Bott, Valentin (SH)

Bouk, Gabriel (HJ)

Bouquet, Henry (R)

Bour, John (R)

Boyer, Valentin (H)

Bracht, E. (K)

Brachvogel, Udo (H)

Brackel, C. W. (K)

Bracken, Charles (HJ)

Braidenback, Henry (R)

Brand, Horace (H)

Brand, Michael (H)

Brand, Rudolph (H)

Brand, Sebastian (HJ, T)

Brandau, H. (H)

Brandecker, C. (K)

Brandeis, Jac. (K)

Brandel, Carl (W)

Brandes, Frederick (H)

Brandt, C. Christian (SH)

Brandt, Carl (H)

Brandt, Ernst (SH)

Brandt, F. W. (SH)

Brandt, Otto (R)

Brandt, Wilhelmina (SH)

Brandwell, Johann (H)

Branick, Joseph (HJ)

Braschler, Johann H. (S)

Bratz, -- (K)

Braun, -- (K)

Braun, Georg (H)

Braun, Pastor Heinrich (GM)

Braun, Bierbrauer (HJ)

Brause, -- von (HJ)

Bredesen, A. (HJ)

Breggy, Louis (R)

Brehm, Derich (R)

Brehm, Dr. E. A. (HJ)

Breidert, -- (K)

Breitmeyer, Philip (R)

Breitschneider, Robert (R)

Breitung, Edward (R)

Bremer, Adolf (G2)

Bremer, Friedericke (K)

Bremer, G. (HJ, K)

Bremer, Henry (R)

Bremer, J. (R)

Bremer, Otto (G2)

Brendecke, -- (K)

Brendecke, Dr. F. (K)

Brentano, Lorenz (H)

Brentano, Theodore (H, R)

Breslauer, Jos. (T)

Brestefeld, Henry (R)

Brettmann, Johann (H)

Bretz, J. Harlan (R)

Breuer, Frank (G2)

Breuhaus, Otto (S)

Breuner, Theodore (G2)

Bricken, Carl (H)

Brickner, Geo. H. (HJ)

Briesen, E. von (HJ)

Briesen E. B. (HJ)

Briggs, Walter (H)

Brinck, Aaron (R)

Brink, Utter (R)

Brinkmann, William (H)

Brinkoff, Dr. -- (HJ)

Britzius, Michael (H)

Brock, Georg (HJ)

Brockelmann, Ernst (HJ)

Brockhauser, Dr. -- (R)

Brockmann, Christophel (SH)

Brockmann, Lewis (SH)

Brockmeyer, Lehrer [teacher] H. D. F. (GM)

Brockschmidt, W. (H)

Broderick, Bertha (A)

Broderick, John (A)

Broderick, Mina (A)

Broderick, Regina (A)

Brög, Chas. J. (K)

Brög, Victorine (K)

Broek, -- van den, Rev. (HJ)

Broockfeld, William (R)

Brosius, A. (K)

Brosius, G. (HJ)

Bross, William (H)

Brown, Anna (SH)

Brown, George (SH)

Brown, Dr. H. M. (T)

Brucker, -- (TC)

Brucker, Ferdinand (R)

Brucker, Gustav (R)

Brucker, Joseph (H, HJ)

Bruckner, Pastor -- (R)

Bruckner, Herman (R)

Bruecker, John (W)

Brueggeman, Frank (R)

Bruehl, L. (K)

Bruening, Hans (HJ)

Brum, Christopher (R)

Brumder, Georg (HJ, T)

Brumder, Wm. C. (T)

Brumme, Carl C. G. (R)

Brun, Anton (H)

Bruner, Charles Theodore (R)

Bruner, Jacob (R)

Bruning, August (H)

Brunken, Ernst (HJ)

Brunner, Henry (H)

Brunnow, Franz Friedrich (R)

Bruno, J. (K)

Brunold, Peter (R)

Bruns, Pastor H. (GM)

Brunschweiler, George L. (R)

Brunst, -- (HJ)

Brunst, G. (K)

Bruske, Rev. August F. (R)

Bruske, Gottlieb (R)

Brust, Anna (SH)

Brust, George (SH)

Brust, Jacob (SH)

Brust, Philipina (SH)

Bry, Theodorus von (G2)

Buchholz, Friedrich (H)

Buchinger-Heringman, Christiane (G2)

Buchmüller, Heinrich (S)

Buck, Daniel (R)

Buck, Florence (R)

Buckelmüller, Heinrich (HJ)

Buckelmüller, M. (K)

Buckner, Jas. (HJ)

Budde, Henry (H)

Buderbach, -- (K)

Buechel, Anton (W)

Buechner, Dr. Ludwig (HJ)

Buehler, -- (R)

Bühler, Curt (H)

Buehler, Edward (H)

Bühler, Johann Jakob (S)

Buehler, John (H)

Buehming, W. (T)

Buehrig, L. H. (S)

Bülow, Hans von (H)

Bues, Frederick (HJ)

Buestrin, Aug.H (T)

Buestrin, Henry F. (T)

Bütow, C. (K)

Buetow, Chas. L. (T)

Buhl, Christian Henry (R)

Buhl, Frederick Augustus (R)

Bulkey, Frank (R)

Bull, Ole (K)

Bunde, L. W. (T)

Bundesen, Hermann (H)

Bunge, Karl (H)

Bunteschu, Wm. (T)

Burdick, P. (K)

Burglund, Paul (H)

Burgo, Clara (A)

Burk, Prof. G. (GM)

Burkhardt, Catherine (R)

Burkhart, Nikolaus (S)

Burkholder, Abraham (R)

Burky, Frederick (H)

Burling, Edward (H)

Burmann, Joseph (W)

Busch, Franz (H)

Busch, John (H)

Busch, John J. (R)

Busch, Valentin (H)

Buschbauer, Hans (H)

Buschbeck, Brig. Gen. -- (HJ)

Buscher, E. (T)

Busse, Fred (H, TC)

Busse, Gustavus (H)

Butterman, Eugene (R)

Butz, Caspar (TC)

Butz, Otto (TC)

Butzel, Magnus (R)

Butzel, Martin R. (R)

Buxa, Gottlieb (A)

Buxa, John (A)

Buxa, Mary (A)

Cahensley, Peter Paul (G1)

Cahn, G. A. (T)

Camber, Emilian (R)

Carree, P. (K)

Carstens, J. H. (E)

Carstens, Dr. John Henry (R)

Carstensen, --- (E)

Carus, F. (HJ)

Caspary, S. (HJ)

Casper, -- (K)

Cassian, F. (K)

Casterlein, Jacob (R)

Castor, Elizabeth (SH)

Castor, Jacob (SH)

Castor, John B. (SH)

Castor, Labella (SH)

Chapman, Alice G. (T)

Charnetski, Laura (A)

Charnetski, Ludwig (A)

Charnetski, Mary (A)

Charnetski, Michael (A)

Charnetski, Minnie (A)

Charnetsky, Minnie (A)

Christ, Michael (W)

Christiansen, -- (K)

Christianson, Christian (HJ)

Christensen, George Luther (R)

Christophel, Angela (SH)

Christophel, Barbara (SH)

Christophel, Henry (SH)

Christophel, John (SH)

Cirkler, Herman (SH)

Cirkler, Johanna (SH)

Claas, A. C. (T)

Clarkmottl, Emma (R)

Clas, Alfred C. (HJ)

Clauder, Jos. (HJ)

Claus, -- (K, R)

Clause, William (R)

Claussen, August (SH)

Claussen, Ernst (E)

Claussen, H. R. (E)

Claussenius, Henry (TC)

Clausing, William (G1)

Clemens, Christian (R)

Cloester, Ottomar (R)

Cloeter, Ernest Ottomar (G2)

Closter, Ottmar (R)

Cohen, Frederick (R)

Cohen, Peter (TC)

Cohn, -- (K)

Cohn, Hugo (T)

Colclazer, Rev. Henry (R)

Colclazer, Jacob (R)

Coleman, E. W. (T)

Coleman, H. H. (T)

Collmer, Julius (HJ)

Comegys, Cornelius (R)

Comstock, Cic. (K)

Conrad, C. E. (S)

Conrad, Charles Frederick (R)

Conrad, John (R)

Conradi, -- (K)

Conradi, George (E)

Conradi, J. Philipp (S)

Conze, Alexander (HJ, K)

Cook/Koch, Anton (W)

Cook/Koch, Casper (W)

Cook/Koch, Catharina (W)

Cook/Koch, Phillip (W)

Corbus, Gottfried (R)

Corbus, Richard (R)

Cordes, Anton Bernard (W)

Cordes, J. H. (K)

Cordes, John (R)

Corselius, George (R)

Cottrell, Henry (R)

Cotzhausen, A. von (T)

Cotzhausen, F. W. von (HJ, T)

Couse, Adam (R)

Couse, E. Anger (R)

Craemer, -- (R)

Craemer, Pastor -- (R)

Crager, Jacob (R)

Cramer, -- (K)

Cramer, Ad. (K)

Cramer, E. (K)

Cramer, E. C. (T)

Cramer, Peter (R)

Cramer, W. P. (T)

Crell, Joseph (R)

Cremer, Henry (R)

Crissman, Michael (R)

Crocker, Hans (K)

Cron, Lt. Anton Caesar (R)

Crone, Gesine (SH)

Crone, Theodore (SH)

Crotz, J. B. (K)

Croul, Jerome (R)

Crouse, Theodore (R)

Curtenius, A. E. (R)

Curtenius, Frederick WIlliam (R)

Custer, Abel (R)

Custer, George Alexander (R)

Custer, Thomas W. (R)

Czak, Louise (A)

Czizek, Augustus (R)

Czudnochowski, Augusta (A)

Czudnochowski, Augusta (A)

Czudnochowski, Bertha (A)

Czudnochowski, Charlotte (A)

Czudnochowski, Fred (A)

Czudnochowski, Frederick (A)

Czudnochowski, Frederick (A)

Czudnochowski, Fredericka (A)

Czudnochowski, Gust (A)

Czudnochowski, Hattie (A)

Czudnochowski, Hattie (A)

Czudnochowski, Heinrich (A)

Czudnochowski, John (A)

Czudnochowski, John (A)

Czudnochowski, John (A)

Czudnochowski, Martha (A)

Czudnochowski, Martha (A)

Czudnochowski, Michael (A)

Czudnochowski, Michael (A)

Czudnochowski, Michael (A)

Czudnochowski, Michael (A)

Czudnochowski, Minnie (A)

Czudnochowski, Minnie (A)

Czudnochowski, Minnie (A)

Czudnochowski, Wilhelm (A)

Dablon, Pastor -- (K)

Dabo, Leon (R)

Dabo, Theodore Scott (R)

Dahlmann, A. (T)

Dahlmann, J. (K)

Damback, Catherine (SH)

Damback, Joseph (SH)

Dames, Wilhelm (HJ)

Damköhler, F. (T)

Dams, Emily (A)

Dams, Emma (A)

Damsky, Adalbert (W)

Danziger, J. C. (R)

Dapprich, Emil (HJ, T)

Daries, Friedrich (S)

Darling, Jasper T. (TC)

Darmstaetter, Jacob (R)

Darmstaetter, William (R)

Dasler, Pastor A. (GM)

Daubert, Karl L. (S)

De Bries, Mdm. -- (K)

De Haas, Dr. Carl (HJ)

De Longuiel, M. (R)

De Low, Rev. Dr. -- (R)

De Peyster, Col. -- (R)

Dederichs, Peter (R)

Degan, Mathias (TC)

Dehn, Johann (SH)

Dehn, Johanna (SH)

Dehne, -- (HJ)

Deierling, -- (K)

Deinard, Rabbi Samuel N. (G2)

Deindorfer, Pastor -- (R)
Dejean, P. S., Rev. (HJ)
Delveau, Friedrich (S)
Delvendahl, -- (K)
Demmer, Lawrence (T)
Denkhaus, John (A)
Depolder, Fidel (SH)
Depolder, Frank (SH)
Depolder, Josephine (SH)
Depolder, Theresa (SH)
Deren, D. Van (HJ, K)
Dessel, H. A. (E)
Dessert, Joseph (HJ)
Dernehl, Paul H. (HJ)
Dernehl, Ulrich (T)
Dethoff, Carl C. (R)
Deuber, Pastor S. (GM)
Deubler, Conrad (HJ)
Deuel, Andrew L. (R)
Deuster, -- (K)
Deuster, Oscar B. (HJ)
Deuster, P. B. (HJ, K)
Deuster, P. V. (T)
Deutsch, Henry (T)
Devens, Chas (HJ)
Dewitt, J. (K)
Deyrenfurth, Julius (TC)
Dick, A. C. (T)
Dickhaus, Prof. Joseph H. (R)
Diddes, Robert (G2)
Diebold, Jerome Heron (W)
Diechman, Ferdinand (R)
Dieckhoff, Thomas Johann (R)
Dieckman, Frederick (R)
Diederichs, -- (K)
Diederichs, E. (K)
Diedrichsen A. (K)
Diefenbach, John (R)
Diegel, Henry (R)
Diehl, Francis (R)
Diemer, Hugo (R)
Dierstein, Samuel (R)
Dietrich, -- (HJ)
Dietrich, Ernst (SH)
Dietrich, Pauline (SH)
Dietsch, -- (TC)
Dietsch, Gustav (E)
Dietsgen, Joseph (TC)
Dietz, Adolph (SH)
Dietz, August (SH)
Dietz, Charlotte (SH)
Dietz, Frederick (SH)

Dietz, George (SH)
Dietz, Henry (SH)
Dietz, Joseph (SH)
Dietz, Margareth (SH)
Dietz, Margaretha (SH)
Dietz, Mary (SH)
Dietz, Theresia (SH)
Diez, Chr. (K)
Diez, Phillip (E)
Dilbeck, -- (R)
Dilger, Hubert (HJ)
Dilg, Wilhelm (HJ)
Dillenback, John (R)
Dillenback, Laura (R)
Dillmann, Adam (HJ, T)
Dippel, Louis (E)
Dirk (Doerk), John (A)
Dirk, John Heinrich (A)
Dirk (Doerk), Marie (A)
Dittbenner, Augusta (SH)
Dittbenner, Louis (SH)
Dittmar, John (R)
Dobbreton, John (R)
Dobrzewsky, Fred (A)
Dock, George (R)
Dodder, Jacob (R)
Doebereiner, Cresentia (SH)
Doebereiner, John A. (SH)
Döhring, Karl F. (S)
Doehrschalg, -- (K)
Doeltz, William (R)
Doer, Chas (E)
Doerflinger, -- (K)
Doerflinger, Carl (HJ, T)
Dohmen, P. L. (HJ)
Doll, Katharina (W)
Domann, Paul (E)
Domitio/Damitio, John (W)
Domschke, Bernhard (HJ, K)
Donges, J. R. (K)
Donner, William (R)
Dopp, Catherine Elizabeth (R)
Dora, John (A)
Dorce, Hattie (A)
Dorestan, Udo (T)
Dorman, August (R)
Dornbach, G. (HJ)
Dorner, Dr. C. Hermann (HJ)
Dorsch, Dr. Edward (R)
Dousman, G. (K)
Dousman, M. (K)
Dousman, Michael (R)

Dousman, T. C. (K)

Dowidat, Pastor P. (GM)

Draz, -- (K)

Dreher, W. F. (E)

Dreitz, Ph. (K)

Dremmel, -- (HJ)

Dremmel, Jul. (K)

Dresel, Theodor H. (S)

Dresen, Louise (K)

Dresen, W. (K)

Dreuillettes, Gabriel (HJ)

Drewel, Friedrich (S)

Drexelius, Frederick (R)

Drexler, Benedict (SH)

Drexler, Margaretha (SH)

Droste, Theodore (W)

Dubendorf, Edward (R)

Duchoslow, J. (K)

Duda, Charlotte (A)

Duda, Jennie (A)

Dudek, Frederick (A)

Dudek, Martha (A)

Dudek, Oscar (A)

Dudenhöfer, Jacob (T)

Duemling, Dr. Hermann (HJ)

Duengle, -- (R)

Dürr, -- (K)

Dürr, J. Louis (S)

Duerst, Balthasar (HJ)

Duerst, Mathias (HJ)

Duerst, Nicholas (HJ)

Duevel, August (SH)

Duevel, Augusta (SH)

Duevel, Franz (SH)

Dueweke, Christina K. (R)

Dueweke, John J. (R)

Duggau, Th. (K)

Dulitz, Pastor -- (K)

Dulitz, Friedrich (S)

Dumser, Pastor Simon (R)

Dunnebacke, Franz A. (W)

Dunnebacke, John Christoph (W)

Dunnebacke, John Joseph (W)

Durege, Dr. -- (HJ, K)

Durenberger, David (G1)

Durki, Minnie (A)

Durr, Emil (HJ)

Durst, August THeodore Benedict (R)

Durward, Brand Isaac (HJ)

Duttlinger, F. (K)

Dyhrenfurth, J. (K)

Dysterheft, Pastor A. J. (GM)

Eberbach, Christian (R)

Eberdt, Pastor Julius (R)

Eberhard, John P. (R)

Eberle, Herman Roth (R)

Eberle, Jacob (R)

Eberle, Phillip (E)

Eberstein, Conrad (R)

Eberstine, Henry (R)

Ebert, -- (K)

Eberts, Dr. Herman Melchior (R)

Eble, -- (K)

Eble, Andreas (HJ)

Ebling, G. (S)

Eckstein, Ad. (HJ)

Eckstein, Caroline (SH)

Eckstein, Henry (SH)

Eddy, Joseph (R)

Edelman, John D. (R)

Eden, John (E)

Edlefsen, Wm. (T)

Edleman (Edelman?), Hattie (A)

Effinger, Rev. Augustine M. (R)

Effinger, John R. (R)

Egan, John (W)

Ege, Dr. -- (R)

Ege, C. N. (R)

Egery, G. A. (HJ)

Eggeman, David Bernhard (R)

Egger, F. (HJ)

Eggert, -- (K)

Eggert, Pastor A. W. (GM)

Eggert, John (R)

Egler, Philip (R)

Ehlebrecht, -- (K)

Ehlers, Ed. (K)

Ehlers, Heinrich (S)

Ehlert, Pastor F. (GM)

Ehrenstrasser, John George (R)

Ehret, Gweo. (HJ)

Ehrhardt, Eugen L. (G2)

Eibler, -- (K)

Eiboeck, Joseph (E)

Eichelsdorfer, William (R)

Eichenberg, William Louis (R)

Eicher, Rev. Michael (R)

Eidlitz, Cyrus W. (R)

Eigner, J. (K)

Eilers, H. (K)

Eilett, Jacob (R)

Eiring, B. H. (T)

Eiring, H. (K)

Eisenach, -- (R)

Eisendraht, D. B. (HJ)

Eisenhauer, A. (S)

Eisfelder, F.G. (HJ)

Eisfeldt, Chas. (HJ)

Eldred, E. (K)

Eldred, Julius (R)

Elias, Edward A. M., Ph.D. (R)

Eller, John (T)

Ellinghausen, H. (T)

Ellmenreich, -- (HJ)

Elmer, Peter Jenz (HJ)

Elser, John (T)

Elsner, Richard (T)

Ely, A. (K)

Ely, Lidia (HJ)

Ely, Prof. R. P. (HJ)

Emerich, William (SH)

Emmel, Pastor A.E.G. (GM)

Emmeric, Joseph (SH)

Emmerling, Dr. F. H. (T)

Emmerling, J. C. (T)

End, A. (K)

End, E. (K)

Ende, Amalie von (HJ)

Ende, Henrik von (HJ)

Enderis, H. W. (T)

Enders, Frank (HJ)

Endlich, John (R)

Endres, F. (K)

Enes, -- (K)

Engbring, Wm. (HJ)

Engdahl, J. Lewis (TC)

Endres, E. F. (T)

Engel, George (TC)

Engel, Pastor J. (GM)

Engel, Johannes (R)

Engel, Pastor Th. (GM)

Engelbach, Johann (S)

Engelbert, Henry (SH)

Engelbert, Rebecca (SH)

Engelhardt, Rev. Zephyrin (R)

Engelmann, J. B. (K)

Engelmann, P. (K)

Engelmann, Peter (HJ)

England, Lina (SH)

England, William (SH)

Engleman, Michael (R)

Enos, S. C. (K)

Eppling, Pastor F. (R)

Eppens, Heinrich A. (S)

Erley, Rev. Hugo J. (R)

Ermatinger, Lawrence (R)

Ermis, John (A)

Ermis, Ludwig (A)

Ermis, Louis (A)

Ermis, William (A)

Ernest, Caspar (R)

Ernst, A. F. (HJ)

Erwin, R. (HJ)

Esch, Engelbert (W)

Esch, Henriette (K)

Esch, Michael ("Papa Esch") (G2)

Eschweiler, F. C. (T)

Eschweiler, Franz Chadbourne (R)

Eskuche, Henry (T)

Eskuche, L. (T)

Esper, Jacob (R)

Esselen, Christian (HJ, K)

Esterly, C. (K)

Etherage, Anna (R)

Etzling, R. (HJ)

Etzlinger, Carl J. (HJ)

Everard, Herbert (R)

Ewald, Louise (A)

Ewalt, Jacob (R)

Eyme, Ludwig (R)

Fabor, Rev. William F. (R)

Failing, Henry (R)

Faist, Wm. (T)

Falckner, -- (R)

Falk, F. R. (T)

Falk, L. W. (T)

Falkstein, John (R)

Fandel, Frank (G2)

Fandel, John (W)

Fandel, Peter (W)

Fangboner, Daniel (R)

Faser, Maria (R)

Fasolt, G. (HJ, K)

Fasquelle, Louis (R)

Fassbind, Franz (G2)

Faulkner, Martin (R)

Fausel, Friedrich (S)

Faust, Albert Bernhard (R)

Fay, Louis (SH)

Fay, Louisa A. (SH)

Federlein, Martin (R)

Federman, Nikolaus (G2)

Federmeyer, -- (K)

Fedewa/Vidua, Adam (W)

Fedewa, John H. (R)

Fedewa, Morris (R)

Fehlinger, C. (HJ)

Fehr, Hermann (HJ)

Feil, J. Christoph (S)

Fekete, S. I. (R)

Feld, Dr. C. (K)

Feldner, Edward (R)

Feldpausch, Franz (W)

Felker, Peter H. (R)

Felsecker, F. J. (HJ, K)

Felter, C. W. (HJ)

Feneis/Fineis, Michael (W)

Fenstermacher, Saul (R)

Ferber, Edna (R)

Ferle, Henry (R)

Fernekes, Emma (T)

Fernekes, Gustave (R)

Fernekes, Val. (T)

Ferners, Joseph (R)

Fernholz, Franz (W)

Fernow, T. (K)

Ferry, Geo. B. (HJ)

Feske, -- (R)

Fessel, Dr. -- (HJ, K)

Fetzer, Peter (HJ)

Feuerhak, George (R)

Feuling, John B. (HJ)

Feutz, Christian G. (S)

Fichtenberg, M. (T)

Fick, B. (HJ)

Fick, Pastor Herman (R)

Fidler, R. (HJ)

Fiebing, Bella (HJ)

Fiebing, Otto (HJ)

Fiebing, O. J. (T)

Fiebrantz, W. H. (HJ)

Fily, L. (K)

Finch, A. Jr. (K)

Finch, B. W. (K)

Finch, Mitz. (K)

Fingado, Chas. (HJ)

Finger, A. (K)

Fink, Bruno (HJ)

Fink, Henry (HJ, T)

Fink, J. (K)

Fink, Martin (SH)

Fink, Max (SH)

Fink, Monica (SH)

Fink, Wilhelm (HJ)

Fink, William (W)

Finkler, A. (T)

Finkler, W. (K)

Finzel, George (R)

Firehaudt, Wilhelm (R)

Firmerich, Ferdinand (W)

Firmilian, Brother -- (R)

Fischbein, J. (K)

Fischer, -- (K)

Fischer, Rev. Dr. -- (TC)

Fischer, Adolph (TC)

Fischer, Anna (SH)

Fischer, Friedrich (E)

Fischer, Pastor G. (GM)

Fischer, Georg (HJ, K)

Fischer, Gotthelf (R)

Fischer, Peter (R)

Fischer, Richard (SH)

Fischer, Richard (R)

Fischer, Theodor (HJ)

Fischer, William (R)

Fisher, Frederick J. (R)

Fisher, John (R)

Fleischauer, Alfred L. (R)

Fleischhacker, J. C. (S)

Fleischmann, -- (HJ)

Fleitz, John P. (R)

Fleming, Wm. (HJ)

Flertzheim, A. (K)

Flertzheim, Ad. (T)

Flesch, --, Bischof (HJ)

Flescheim, Joseph (R)

Flick, Jacob T. (SH)

Flick, Louise (SH)

Flinterman, Johann (R)

Flinterman, Rudolph F. (R)

Flugel, Charles (R)

Foerster, Erwin (T)

Förster, Pfarrer Peter (F)

Follen, Karl (HJ)

Follen, Paul (HJ)

Folz, Leroy Stewart (R)

Forster, Alois (SH)

Forster, Cecilia (SH)

Forster, Frederick (SH)

Forster, Margaretta (SH)

Fortwinkler, Henry (SH)

Fotsch, Martin (S)

Fox/Fuchs, Anton (W)

Fox/Fuchs, Johann (W)

Frahm, Mathias (E)

Fralick, Henry (R)

Fralick, Peter (R)

Frambach, H. A. (R)

Francis, Peter (R)

Frank, A. (K)

Frank, August Friedrich (F)

Frank, Ernst (F)

Frank, H. O. (HJ, T)

Frank, Heinrich Gustav (F)

Frank, Pfarrer Johann Heinrich (F)

Frank, John (R)

Frank, John H. (T)

Frank, John Peter (R)

Frank, Joseph Franz (E)

Frank, Jul. O. (T)

Frank, Dr. Louis F. (T)

Franke, Emil Arthur (R)

Frankfurt[h], William (HJ, K)

Frankfurt[h], Frau W. (HJ)

Frankhauser, Wm. H. (R)

Frappe, Martin (R)

Fratny, Friedrich (HJ, K)

Frattinger, Peter (HJ, K)

Fredenburg, John (R)

Fredenburg, Sylvester (R)

Freer, Paul C. (R)

Freideman, Otto Herman (R)

Freidhoff, John (R)

Freitag, Rev. R. J. (HJ)

Freivalt, Anne (A)

Freivalt, Frederick (A)

Freivalt, Gustave (A)

Freivalt (?), Louisa (A)

Frelinghuysen, Gen. Frederick (R)

Frelinhuysen, Rev. Theo. J. (R)

Frensdorf, Edward (R)

Freund, H. (K)

Freund, Katharine (W)

Freund, Quirin (W)

Frey, Lehrer [teacher] H. (GM)

Frey, Dorothy (T)

Frey, F. J. (T)

Frey, Gottlieb (R)

Frey, John Michael (W)

Frey, Theo. (T)

Freyhofer, Louise (R)

Freytag, Gustav (HJ)

Frick, Elias (SH)

Frick, Mary (SH)

Fricke, A. (HJ)

Fricke, Chas. (HJ)

Fricke, Chas. F. (T)

Fricke, W. A. (HJ)

Friday, John (E)

Friedberg, Jos. (T)

Friedberg, Sam. E. (T)

Frieden, John Peter (R)

Friedland, John F. (R)

Friedmann, Ignatz (HJ)

Friend, D. H. (T)

Friend, J. G. (HJ)

Friend, Elias (HJ)

Friese, Minna (K)

Frieseke, Frederick (R)

Frieseke, Frederick Carl N. A. (R)

Friess, -- (R)

Friess, Johann Georgwe (R)

Friton, August (SH)

Friton, German (SH)

Friton, Johanna (SH)

Friton, John P. (SH)

Friton, Maria (SH)

Friton, Maria Anna (SH)

Friton, Max (SH)

Fritsche, Ernst (SH)

Fritsche, Frederica (SH)

Fritsche, Fred (SH)

Fritsche, Fritz (SH)

Fritsche, Karl (SH)

Fritsche, Dr. L. A. (G2)

Fritsche, Dr. Louis (G1)

Fritz, Pastor E. G. (GM)

Fritz, John (R)

Fritz, M. J. (R)

Fritz, Theodor (HJ)

Fritzle, Pastor, G. E. (GM)

Froebes, Prof. John B. (R)

Froedert, Wm. (T)

Froehlich, Paul E. (T)

Fröhlich, W. H. (HJ)

Frogensus, Brother -- (R)

Frohbach, A. (T)

Frohne, Philipp (S)

Fromm, Wilhelm (S)

Frorib, Dorthea (SH)

Frorib, Maria (SH)

Frorib, Maria (SH)

Frost, L. (HJ)

Frudden, H. F. (E)

Frue, Captain W. B. (R)

Fuchs, [Dr.] J. P. (HJ, K)

Fülle, Karl (HJ, K)

Fuerbringer, Louis Ernest (R)

Fürst, -- (HJ)

Funk, -- (K)

Funke, Moses A. (R)

Furbeck, John Phillip (R)

Furmann, A. (K)

Fusz, Prof. Vincent A. (R)

Gackenheimer, David (S)

Gag, Barbara (SH)

Gag, John G. (SH)

Gag, Maria (SH)

Gag, Peter (SH)

Galich, Theod. (E)

Galinsky, Hans (G2)

Gall, Ludwig (G2)

Gall, Peter (R)

Galles, Anna (SH)

Galles, William (SH)

Gallun, A. F. (HJ)

Galster, Matthias (S)

Garfide, B. (HJ)

Garlichs, Hermann (S)

Gartner, George (R)

Gassman, Ernestina (SH)

Gassman, John (SH)

Gass/Goss, Adam (W)

Gasser, J. M. (K)

Gast, Bernhard (W)

Gausewitz, Pastor, Carl F. W. (GM)

Gauss, Christian (R)

Gebhard, Anna (SH)

Gebhard, Joseph (SH)

Gebser, Berta (SH)

Gebser, William J. (SH)

Gedicke, Pastor P. (GM)

Gehm, Pastor, J. C. A. (GM)

Gehr, Pastor -- (K)

Gehrig, Lou (G2)

Gehrig, Joseph (E)

Gehrine, Rev. Henry (R)

Gehring, Herbert August (R)

Geiger, Benjamin F. (R)

Geik, Nicholas (R)

Geilfuss, A. B. (T)

Geilfuß, Albert (HJ)

Geilfuß, F. (K)

Geisberg, C. (HJ, K)

Geise, Conrad (E)

Geisen, Frank (R)

Geisler, R. J. (E)

Geissmor, Henry (R)

Geitel, Andreas (HJ)

Geller, Ferdinand (W)

Geller, John Joseph (W)

Gellert, Johannes Sophus (R)

Gentner, Louis Gustav (R)

Gephart, Capt. Henry (R)

Georg, Theodor (HJ)

George, D. (HJ, K)

George, P. J. (K)

Gerber, B. (H)

Gerber, Johannes (S)

Gehrhardt, Paul (H)

Gerlach, Christian (R)

Gerlach, Mar. (HJ, K)

Gerlach, Theodore (W)

Gerloff, Augusta (A)

German[n], F. (H, HJ, K)

Germer, Adolph (H, TC)

Gerst, Francis J. (R)

Gerstenhauer, Eugene (SH)

Gerstenhauer, Louisa (SH)

Gerts, John (H)

Geser, -- (K)

Getman, George Arnold (R)

Gettelmann, A. (HJ, T)

Gettering, Winnifred Sarah (R)

Gettman, Solomon (R)

Getzler, Anton (H)

Geuder, Wm. (HJ, T)

Geyer, Pastor -- (K)

Geyser, Prof. Anthony F. (R)

Gherken, Heinrich (H)

Giebel, C. K. (HJ)

Giegold, Georg (HJ)

Gies, Jacob (R)

Gies, John H. (R)

Gies, Joseph (R)

Gies, Joseph (H)

Gies, Joseph W. (R)

Gies, Lorenz (R)

Gies, Paul (R)

Gies, Paul (R)

Gies, Wilhelm (R)

Gieschen, Lehrer [teacher] Claus (GM)

Giese, W. F. (HJ)

Giesler, A. C. (HJ)

Giesler, Julius (HJ)

Giesmann, -- (K)

Gieseler, Frln. [Ms.] (K)

Gieseler, K. (K)

Gilowsky, Jos. (T)

Ginal, Heinrich (HJ, K)

Gindele, John (H)

Ginsterblum/Gensterblum, Anton (W)

Gintz, J. (K)

Girten, Michael (H)

Gissible, Fritz (H)

Glade, Hermann (H)

Glaessner, Georg (H)

Glambock, Johann (H)

Glanz, Louis (H)

Glasen, Johann (H)

Glaser, Emil (R)

Glatz, R. (K)

Glecker, Adolph (TC)

Glick, Dr. George (E)

Glogauer, Fritz (H)

Glogoener, Fritz (TC)

Glos, Johann (H)

Gluth, Amasia (SH)

Gluth, Stephen (SH)

Gmeiner, John (HJ)

Goblicki, Jennie (A)

Godeke, Wilhelm (R)

Godez, Peter (R)

Goebel, August (R)

Göbel, Johann Peter (S)

Goebel, Julius (H)

Goebel, Peter (T)

Göbel, Philipp (S)

Goeden, Susan (H)

Goedert/Gaedert, Phillip (W)

Gögg, Amand (K)

Goelzer, Daniel (HJ)

Goeppert-Mayer, Maria (H)

Goerge, Anton (W)

Goerge, Edward (W)

Goerge, John (W)

Gös, F. (K)

Goes, G. (T)

Goetchius, Steven (R)

Göth, -- (K)

Goetsch, Henry Max (R)

Götsch, J. (K)

Göttig, H. C. (K)

Goetz, Christian (R)

Götz, W. (K)

Götzler, Franz (HJ)

Goldmann, Ferdinand (HJ)

Goldschmidt, Julius (HJ)

Goldsmith, John (R)

Goldzier, Julius (TC)

Goll, F. T. (T)

Goll, Julius (F, K)

Goltke, Christian (SH)

Goltke, Sophie (SH)

Gomberg, Moses (R)

Gonner, Nicklaus, Sr. (E)

Gonner, Ric. (HJ)

Goodmann/Gutmann, Christian Anthony (W)

Goos, Valentine (R)

Gorder, William (HJ)

Gore, Martha (A)

Gorenflo, Theodore (R)

Goroncy, Catherine (A)

Gortz, Joseph (R)

Gosch, Hans (K)

Goschen, J. R. (HJ)

Gosiger, Rev. Frederick A. (R)

Gott, James B. (R)

Gottfried, A. (H)

Gottig, Kurt (H)

Grabau, Rev. -- (HJ, K)

Grabau, Johannes (HJ)

Gradle, Heinrich (H)

Graebner, -- (R)

Graebner, Pastor -- (R)

Graebner, Alan (G2)

Graebner, H. (HJ)

Graebner, John Henry Phillip (R)

Graefe, Martin (G2)

Graenicher, Dr. S. (HJ)

Graeser, Dr. B. (E)

Graetz, Oscar (HJ)

Graeverat, Garret (R)

Graf, -- (R)

Graf, C. A. (T)

Graf, W. L. J. (T)

Graf, Wm. (T)

Graff, John (SH)

Graff, Katharine (SH)

Graffenried, Baron Christ. (R)

Grafley, Charles (R)

Grahl, Gustav (HJ, K)

Grahn, Robert (R)

Gram, C. (HJ)

Gram, Ed. (T)

Grammer, -- (K)

Granacher, -- (K)

Grasty, Charles (H)

Gratzler, M. (K)

Grau, M. (K)

Grau, Wm. H. (T)

Graue, Friedrich (H)

Graul, Charles (R)

Greiner, Michael (R)

Grell, Paul (A)

Grelling, Gotlieb (R)

Greenebaum, Elias (H)

Greenebaum, Henry (H)

Greifenhagen, Karl (H)

Grenshky, Peter (R)

Gres, Henry (R)

Grese, Albert A. (E)

Gretsch, Fred (H)

Gretsch, John (SH)

Gretsch, Joseph (SH)

Gretsch, Margaret (SH)

Gretsch, Theresia (SH)

Grettenberger, Marion Louise (R)

Greulich, August (HJ, K)

Greulich, F. (HJ)

Greusel, -- (R)

Greusel, John (R)

Greusel, Joseph (R)

Greusel, Nicholas (R)

Greusel, Nicholas, Jr. (R)

Greve, J. H. (K)

Griebling, O. (T)

Griem, -- (HJ)

Grimm, -- (HJ)

Grimm, Lehrer [teacher] F. (GM)

Grimm, Peter (R)

Grimm, Wendelin (G1, G2)

Grimmelsman, Rev. Joseph F. X. (R)

Grimmie, Fred (H)

Grinnell, Julius E. (TC)

Gritzon, August (A)

Gritzon, Frederick (A)

Groenlund, Lawrence (HJ)

Groesbeck, Alex J. (R)

Groesbeck, Walter D. (R)

Groll, John (R)

Groll, Philipp (H)

Grones, Joseph (W)

Groneweg, Wm. (E)

Groninger, Hugo (E)

Gross, Agnes (A)

Gross, August (A)

Gross, Carl Gustav (A)

Gross, F. C. (T)

Gross, Fred (A)

Gross, Frederick (A)

Gross, Georg (H)

Gross, Henry (H)

Gross, Jacob (H)

Gross, John (W)

Gross, Mathias (W)

Gross, Michael (W)

Gross, Michael (W)

Gross, Peter (W)

Gross, S. E. (H)

Gross, Theodor (H)

Grosse, August (A)

Grosse, Charles (A)

Grosse, Edward (A)

Grosse, Gustave (A)

Grosse, Wilhelmina (A)

Grossenbach, G. (T)

Grossenbach, R. L. (T)

Grossman, Jennie (A)

Grossman, Rabbi Louis (R)

Groß, J. P. (K)

Großmann, G. A. (E)

Grote, Heinrich (S)

Grotkie, C. (K)

Grottkau, Paul (H, HJ, TC)

Grotzwink, -- (HJ)

Gruber, Lehrer [teacher] F. (GM)

Gruber, G. (K)

Gruber, Lehrer [teacher] Jm. (GM)

Gründel, C. (K)

Grünewald, -- (K)

Grünfeld, Betty (K)

Grünhagen, -- (K)

Gruenhut, Joseph (H)

Gruening, -- (HJ)

Gruenist, Joseph (R)

Gruenthamer, Prof. M. J. (R)

Grundhofer, Joseph (H)

Gruppe, Carl Paul (R)

Gubler, Jakob (S)

Guck, Homer A. (R)

Gudden, Sophie (HJ)

Guebner, Georg F. (S)

Guensel, Alfred (H)

Günther, Aug. (K)

Günther, Caroline (K)

Gienther, Frederick (R)

Günther, Dr. G. (K)

Guenther, Dr. O. (HJ)

Guenther, Richard (HJ)

Guentzel, G. (HJ)

Guenzel, Louis (H, TC)

Güterbock, Hans (H)

Guetling, Julius (SH)

Guetling, Josephine (SH)

Guetling, Maria (SH)

Guetling, William (SH)

Gugler, Julius (H, HJ, T)

Guiske, Fred H. (E)

Gulch, -- (R)

Gulden, Maria (SH)

Gulden, Nicolas (SH)

Gulden, Robert (SH)

Guldenstein, -- (R)

Gulick, Robert F. (R)

Gundlitz, C. (K)

Gundrum, Frederick (R)

Gunsaulus, F. W. (H)

Gunther, Charles (H)

Gupta, H. L. (TC)

Guse, Pastor J. (GM)

Guseck, Minnie (A)

Guseck, Minnie (A)

Gusick, Jennie (A)

Gusick, John (A)

Gusick, Lizzie (A)

Gusick, Louise (A)

Gusick, Minnie (A)

Gusick, Regina (A)

Guth, Frederick (R)

Guthe, Karl Eugene (R)

Gutmann, Fr. (K)

Guttmann, -- (HJ)

Guzek, Frederick (A)

Guzek, Jacob (A)

Gwinnder, Jacob P. (R)

Haack, C. Gottlieb (S)

Haag, Christian (SH)

Haag, Dorthea (SH)

Haanel, Charles Francis (R)

Haanel, Eugene Emil Felix Richard (R)

Haar, Pastor W. (GM)

Haaren, Franz (E)

Haarer, John W. (R)

Haas, Adam (R)

Haas, C. de (K)

Haas, Christian (S)

Haas, George (SH)

Haas, Gustav (HJ)

Haas, J. F. (H)

Haas, Jacob (R)

Haas, Solomon (H)

Haas, Wilhelm (H)

Haas, Karl De (HJ)

Haase, Pastor G. C. (GM)

Haass, Julius H. (R)

Haben, Andrew (HJ)

Habenbach, Aaron (R)

Haberkorn, -- (K)

Haberkorn, John H. (R)

Hack, Bernard (R)

Hack, John (R)

Hackenberg, -- (R)

Hackendahl, Chr. (K)

Hackman, -- (R)

Haderlein, John (H)

Haeberle, David (SH)

Haeberle, Dorthea (SH)

Haeberle, Leonhard (SH)

Häberle, Louis F. (S)

Härdtle, Johann (S)

Haering, Theodor (H)

Haerling, Gustav (E)

Haertel, Hermann (HJ, K)

Härtel, Oscar (K)

Haettstadt, George William (R)

Hafner/Haefner, Joseph (W)

Hage, Conrad (R)

Hager, Daniel (R)

Hagemann, Eduard (E)

Hagemann, Gustav (S)

Hagenmiller, John (G2)

Hagerman, Franz Heinrich (R)

Hagerman, John (R)

Hahn, F. (H)

Hahn, Georg (HJ)

Hahn, J. F. (R)

Hahn, J. G. (K)

Hahnen, Henry (E)

Haigle, Charles Edmund (R)

Hailmann, W. R. (HJ)

Haise, -- (HJ)

Haist, Adam (E)

Hake, F. D. (T)

Hake, William (R)

Hallacher, Joseph (H)

Halatz, C. (K)

Hale, P. C. (K)

Halfmann, Joseph (W)

Halfmann, Peter Joseph (W)

Hallatz, Charles (HJ)

Halle, E. G. (H)

Haller, Henry C. (R)

Hambach, Henry (R)

Hambach, Jacob D. (R)

Hambach, William (R)

Hambitzer, Joseph F. (R)

Hambitzer, St. J. (K)

Haminski, Michael (R)

Hamm, Edgar (R)

Hammar, Heinrich (SH)

Hammer, -- (K)

Hammer, Charles (R)

Hammer, Clemens (R)

Hammer, Magdaline (SH)

Hammerschlag, S. (T)

Hamtramck, John Francis, Jr. (R)

Hand, Johnny (H)

Hands, William (R)

Hanisch, Max (H)

Hans, Jacob P. (R)

Hansch, H. (K)

Hanschke, J. (K)

Hansen, Bernhard (H)

Hansen, Georg (H)

Hansen, G. J. (T)

Hansen, J. E. (HJ, T)

Hansen, Nels (H)

Hansen, O. C. (T)

Hansen, T. L. (T)

Hanses, John Hermann (W)

Hansing, Charles (SH)

Hantzsch, Robt. A. (T)

Haraßthy, Augustin (HJ, K)

Harbach, Fred (E)

Harbach, Phillip (E)

Hardenburg, Jeremiah (R)

Hardenburg, Louis Martin (R)

Hardy, Edwin L. (R)

Harliman, Peter (R)

Harmann, A. (K)

Harmann, William (H)

Harmer, H. (H)

Harmeyer, August (HJ, K)

Harmeyer, Franz (HJ)

Harmeyer, Heinrich (HJ)

Harnischfeger, H. (T)

Harpcke, H. (K)

Harpfy, Dr. William (R)

Harsens, Bernardus (R)

Harsens, Jacob (R)

Hart, Harry (H)

Hartenbauer, John (E)

Hartert, G. (HJ)

Hartig, Charlotte (T)

Hartke, Christ. (T)

Hartman, Augusta (SH)

Hartman, Frederick (R)

Hartman, Grethe (SH)

Hartman, Henry (SH)

Hartman, Henry (SH)

Hartman, J. (K)

Hartman, John (SH)

Hartman, John H. (SH)

Hartman, Margaretta (SH)

Hartman, Mary Ann (SH)

Hartman, Sergeant (R)

Hartmann, -- (HJ, K)

Hartmann, F. W. (T)

Hartmann, Joseph (H)

Hartmann, Sophus (H)

Hartneck, Joseph (SH)

Hartneck, Rosina (SH)

Hartnetz, L. B. (K)

Harts, Prof. Martin (R)

Hartscher, Francis (R)

Hartsig, John (R)

Harttert, G. (K)

Hartung, G. (K)

Hartwig, Dr. -- (K)

Hartzell, Susanna (R)

Hartzell, Thomas (H)

Hase, -- (HJ)

Hass/Haase, Daniel (W)

Hasse, C. E. (HJ)

Hasse, E. (K)

Hasselman, James Blood (R)

Hasslinger, Martin (R)

Hatala, Aloys (H)

Hatten, W.H. (HJ)

Hattstadt, John James (R)

Hattstaedt, Pastor -- (R)

Hauck, John Phillip (W)

Hauenstein, John (SH)

Hauert, William (H)

Haupt, Lt. Lewis M. (R)

Haupt, Ulrich (H)

Hauser, Hubert (W)

Hauser, Joseph (SH)

Hauser, Maria (SH)

Hausman, Adolph (SH)

Haussner, Carl (H)

Heberlein, Herman (R)

Hecht, Ben (H)

Hecht, David (T)

Heckenberger, -- (K)

Hecker, Frank J. (R)

Hecker, Col. Frank J. (R)

Hecker, Peter (HJ)

Hecker, Fredrick (H, TC)

Heckert, Benjamin F. (R)

Heckert, Fred (SH)

Heckert, Louisa (SH)

Heen, Charles G. (SH)

Heer, J. F. (E)

Heers, Carl (SH)

Heers, Dora (SH)

Heers, Frederick (SH)

Heers, Wm. (SH)

Hefti, Fridolin (HJ)

Heftler, V. R. (R)

Hehl, Sempert (W)

Heibisch, Martin R. (R)

Heide, Hans (K)

Heide, Richard (H)

Heidinger, George Michael (W)

Heidmann, Pastor Robert (GM)

Heil, Casper (E)

Heimerdinger, John (SH)

Heimerdinger, Mary Ann (SH)

Heimsch, -- (R)

Hein, August (SH)

Hein, Caroline (SH)

Hein, Hermann (H)

Heine, Charles (R)

Heine, F. W. (HJ)

Heinebach, Berg (SH)

Heinebach, Justine (SH)

Heineman, Emil S. (R)

Heinemann, G. H. (T)

Heinemann, Geo. H. (HJ)

Heiner, Georg (H)

Heinlein, George Frederick (W)

Heinrich, Christian (R)

Heinrich, E. J. (K)

Heinrichs, Georg (H)

Heins, Henry (E)

Heinsohn, J. A. (K)

Heintz, -- (R)

Heintzen, Jacob (R)

Heintzleman, Samuel (R)

Heintzman, Charles (R)

Heintzman, Christ. (R)

Heinz, Emma (SH)

Heinz, F. (H)

Heinz, John (SH)

Heinzen, Karl (HJ, K, TC)

Heirman, Prof. Francis (R)

Heisel, Adolph (A)

Heisel, Amelia (A)

Heisel, Frederick (A)

Heisel, Gustav (A)

Heisel, Gustav (A)

Heisel, John (A)

Heisel, Ludwig (A)

Heisel, Ludwig (A)

Heisel, Martha (A)

Heisel, Mary (A)

Heisel, Minnie (A)

Heisel (?), Mollie (A)

Heisel, Otto (A)

Heisel, Rhinehold (A)

Heisrodt, Thomas (R)

Heiss, John (R)

Heitkamp, Father Aloysius (R)

Heitlaud, Freda A. M. (R)

Heitz, --, Erzbischof (HJ)

Heitz, Michael (HJ, K)

Heitzelmann, P. (K)

Helfenstein, J. P. (K)

Helfer, Pastor -- (K)

Hellberg, L. (K)

Heller, P. (K)

Heller, Peter (SH)

Heller, S. (T)

Heller, Susan (SH)

Hellmann, William (SH)

Hellmarice, August (SH)

Hellmarice, Sophia (SH)

Helm, J. (K)

Helm, Linai T. (H)

Helmholtz, August C. (HJ, T)

Helmuth, Dr. -- (TC)

Helmuth, Karl (H)

Helwig, Charles (R)

Helwig, George Frank (R)

Helwig, Louisa (R)

Hemje, -- (K)

Hempel, C. (H)

Hempel, J. G. (E)

Hendrick, --, Senator (HJ)

Hemmeter John G. (R)

Hempl, George (R)

Hench, George A. (R)

Henes, John (R)

Henes, Louis (HJ, K)

Henes, Louis, Jr. (T)

Hengel, -- (HJ)

Hengesbach, William (W)

Henk, Anthony (R)

Henkel, Geo. (HJ)

Henkel, Joseph (R)

Henkel, Peter (R)

Henle, Anton (G2)

Henle, Anton (SH)

Henle, Athanaus (SH)

Henle, Therese (SH)

Henn, Edward (R)

Hennecke, Caspar (HJ)

Hennepin, Father -- (R)

Henni, --, Erzbischof (HJ, K)

Henni, Johann Martin (HJ)

Hensler, C. (R)

Henzel, Herman (R)

Herbold, Alexander (HJ)
Herbst, -- (R)
Herbst, S. C. (HJ, T)
Hercz, Arthur (H)
Herfurth, Sabine (HJ)
Herman, August (R)
Herman, H. (T)
Herman, John (R)
Herman, Joseph (R)
Hermann, Adolph (E)
Hermann, John (E)
Hermann, Joseph (SH)
Hermaringer, H. (HJ)
Hermeling, John (R)
Herndorfer, Hermann (SH)
Herndorfer, Louisa (SH)
Herpolsheimer, William G. (R)
Herr/Harr, Bartholomew (W)
Herres, Mathias (W)
Herres, Dr. Simon (W)
Herrlich, Theodor (HJ)
Herrick, -- (HJ)
Herrmann, -- (K)
Hermann, Raphael (R)
Hertle, Daniel (TC)
Herting, John (H)
Herzberg, E. (K)
Herzberg, E. A. (T)
Herzer, -- (HJ)
Herzer, Rev. -- (G2)
Herzer, Rev. John (HJ)
Herzog, Daniel (A)
Herzog, Maximilian (H)
Herzog, Reinhold (A)
Hesing, Anton C. (H, TC)
Hesing, Washington (H, TC)
Hess, Julius (R)
Hess, Peter (R)
Hesse, -- (R)
Hesse, A. B. (T)
Hesse, Bernhardt (R)
Hesse, G. (HJ)
Hesselbach, Otto (H)
Hessert, Gustav (H)
Hest, A. von (K)
Hettinger, A. (H)
Hetz, -- (K)
Hetz, F. John (R)
Heun, Franz (H)
Heyde, -- (K)
Heyde, Claus (K)
Heydenburk, Martin (R)

Heydlauff, Christian (R)

Heydrich, Mary (SH)

Heyer/Heier, August (W)

Heyer, H. L. (K)

Heyer, Johann (G2)

Heyer, Philipp J. (S)

Heyerman, Samuel P. (R)

Heyerstadt, Francis von (G2)

Heyl, Friederika Margretha (R)

Heyl, Jacob (T)

Heymann, F.T. (H)

Heyn, Emil (R)

Heyn, Her. (T)

Heynen, Carl (H)

Hibbeln, Francis (W)

Hickler, Simon (HJ)

Hiecke, Chr. (K)

Hielscher, Theodor (H)

Hientz, Louis (H)

Hiesrodt, John M. (R)

Hilbert, H. J. (HJ, T)

Hilbert, P. A. (G1)

Hilbert, P. (K)

Hild, Frederick (H)

Hildebrand, Charlotte (R)

Hildebrand, Frederick (H)

Hildebrand, G. F. (HJ)

Hildebrand, Wm. (HJ)

Hildebrandt, Dr. -- (HJ)

Hildebrandt, Bernard (R)

Hildesheim, Arnold (SH)

Hildesheim, Clara (SH)

Hildesheim, Henry (SH)

Hildesheim, Hubert (SH)

Hildesheim, Joseph (SH)

Hildesheim, M. Catharine (SH)

Hildner, Johann Augustus Charles (R)

Hildor, Walter Gotlob (R)

Hildreth, James (H)

Hilgard, Eugene Woldemar (R)

Hilgen, F. (HJ, K)

Hilgen, H. (HJ)

Hiller, John D. (SH)

Hiller, Louisa (SH)

Hiller, Peter (R)

Hillgaertner, -- (TC)

Hillgaertner, Georg (H)

Hilman, Frederick H. (R)

Hillmer, M. (K)

Hillmantel, H. (K)

Hilmer, Aug. (E)

Hilsendegen, Valentine (R)

Himmelberger, Ransom (R)
Himmelein, Linde Louise (R)
Himsl, J. B. (G2)
Hindermann, Jacob (SH)
Hindermann, Minna (SH)
Hinderer, Pastor P. (GM)
Hinman, S. (K)
Hinnenthal, Pastor G. (GM)
Hinze, Therese (HJ, K)
Hippolt, Klinger G. (SH)
Hippolt, Mary Ann (SH)
Hirsch, A. M. (H)
Hirsch, Emil G. (H, TC)
Hirsch, H. (T)
Hirschberg, Pauline (T)
Hirschman, Andrew (R)
Hislop, Th. (K)
Hock, -- (R)
Hockhauser, Anton (SH)
Hockhauser, Catharina (SH)
Hoechster, Emil (H)
Höfer, Heinrich (S)
Hoeffer, Rev. George A. (R)
Hoeffgen, Robert (H, TC)
Hoeffler,-- (HJ)
Höger, J. B. (K)
Hoehn, -- (HJ, K)
Hoerl, Henry (T)
Hoellen, John (H)
Hoesli, Fridolin (HJ)
Hoesli, Henry (HJ)
Hoesli, Markus (HJ)
Hoesli, Mathias (HJ)
Hoexter, Prof. Samuel J. (R)
Hofacker, Erich P. (G2)
Hoff, S. H. (T)
Hoffbauer, F. (E)
Hoffbauer, H. (E)
Hoffbauer, Dr. M. (TC)
Hoffend, Prof. Wm. M. (R)
Hoffman, Charles (SH)
Hoffman, George (R)
Hoffman, George W. (R)
Hoffman, Henry (SH)
Hoffman, John D. (R)
Hoffman, Margaret (SH)
Hoffman, Margarita (SH)
Hoffman, Michael (R)
Hoffman, Paul (R)
Hoffman, Peter (R)
Hoffman, Philip H. (R)
Hoffmann, -- (HJ)

Hoffmann, Anna (W)

Hoffmann, B. (HJ)

Hoffmann brothers (H)

Hoffmann, Rev. B. (E)

Hoffmann, B. (T)

Hoffmann, E. (K)

Hoffmann, Emil O. (T)

Hoffmann, Francis (H, HJ)

Hoffmann, Pastor Friedrich (GM)

Hoffmann, Gustav (H)

Hoffmann, H. B. (H)

Hoffmann, J. (K)

Hoffmann, John (T)

Hoffmann, Michael (H)

Hoffmann, Oscar B. (E)

Hoffmann, Oscar (H)

Hoffmann, Wm. (T)

Hoffmeister, Karl (S)

Hofmann, John (H)

Hofsteller, Christ. (R)

Hohenstein, George (SH)

Holinger, Jacques (H)

Holl, Christian (H)

Holl, Franz (SH)

Holl, Franziska (SH)

Hollen, Bernhard von (H)

Hollenbeck, Georg (H)

Hollenberg, Henry (R)

Hollitzer, D. S. (K)

Holm, Barbara (SH)

Holm, John (SH)

Holm, Joseph (SH)

Holmich, Amandus (R)

Holst, B. P. (E)

Holst, Hermann von (H)

Holte, John (H)

Holterhof, Clara (G2)

Holtslander, Joseph (R)

Holzheimer, William Andrew (R)

Holzinger, Lehrer [teacher] K. (GM)

Homeier, Wilhelm (S)

Hommel, -- (R)

Hondorf, John (H)

Honeck, Anthony A. (R)

Hoppes, Mathias (W)

Hopphan, Karl Ernest (R)

Horger, John (R)

Horn, Fred. (HJ)

Horn, Friedrich Wilhelm (HJ, K)

Horn, Fritz (H)

Horn, Jacob (W)

Horn, John van (H)

Hornbach, John (HJ)
Horner, C. (HJ)
Horner, Henry (H)
Hornesser, C. (K)
Hornschuh, A. (T)
Horwitz, -- (HJ, K)
Hosmer, A. S. (K)
Host, -- (HJ)
Hotaling, -- (K)
Hottelmann, -- (HJ)
Hotz, Ferdinand (H)
Hotz, J. J. (S)
Hotz, Karl (H)
Hotzfeld, E. (K)
Houk, Henry (R)
Hoyer, H. (K)
Hoyt, Frank W. (HJ)
Hubbel, L. (K)
Huber, Andreas (R)
Huber, Gotthelf (R)
Huber, H. (K)
Hubinger, Lorenz (R)
Huchting, F. B. (HJ, T)
Huck, Clara (HJ)
Huck, John A. (H)
Huck, Louis C. (H)
Huebschmann, Dr. -- (HJ, K)
Hueffmeier, Johann (H)
Huegin, A. (T)
Huegli, John A. (R)
Huehn, Anna (H)
Huene, Aug. (E)
Huenert, George (R)
Huerman, Prof. Henry G. (R)
Hüstmann, -- (K)
Huetteman, Frank (R)
Huetwald, Frederick (R)
Hufnagel, Anthony (W)
Huhn, Adam (H)
Huhn, Heinrich (HJ)
Huhn, Lorenz (W)
Huglin, G. J. (E)
Hulett, George Augustus (R)
Hulick, Dietrich (R)
Humbert, Jacob (R)
Humell, Margaret (R)
Hummel, Appollonia (SH)
Hummel, Ernst (H)
Hummel, William (SH)
Hundt, Franz (W)
Hunkel, Emil P. (T)
Hunsicker, Silvanus (R)

Hunziker, Pastor J. J. (GM)

Huperz, Christopher (R)

Hupfer, Pastor H. (GM)

Hurd, Genova (SH)

Hurd, Paul (SH)

Hurz, Carl (R)

Hussen, E. (K)

Hustis, J. (K)

Huth, C.F.M. (HJ)

Hutten, Philipp von (G2)

Huttenlocher, J. G (E)

Hutzel, Titus (R)

Hyde, Wm. F. (T)

Hyer, G. (K)

Hyer, R. F. (K)

Igenfritz, Isaac E. (R)

Ihlhardt, Herm. (HJ)

Ihling, Otto (R)

Ihm, Hermann (E)

Ill, Lorenz (E)

Illies, -- (K)

Illing, C. H. (H)

Ilsley, C. F. (T)

Ilsley, G. (K)

Imholte, John (G2)

Immel, -- (R)

Immler, F. A. (HJ)

Inbusch, A. E. (T)

Inbusch, F. H. (HJ, K)

Inbusch, H. G. (T)

Inbusch, W. H. (T)

Inselman, Claus (R)

Insull, Samuel (H)

Ippel, Charles (H)

Ips, John H. (SH)

Ips, Maria (SH)

Irion, Andreas (S)

Irkenbach, John (R)

Irrer, Sebastian (W)

Irwin, S. (H)

Isenstein, Georg (H)

Isermann, Haino (H)

Israel, Magnus (R)

Iversen, J. C. (T)

Jachinski, Mary Borkowski (A)

Jacker, Edward (R)

Jacob, Homer (R)

Jacobi, -- (HJ)

Jacobi, Fritz (TC)

Jacobi, W. T. (T)

Jacobs, Carl (SH)

Jacobs, Christopher (R)

Jacobs, George (SH)

Jacobs, Hirma (R)

Jacobs, Louis (R)

Jacobs, Louisa (SH)

Jacobs, W. H. (T)

Jacobs, Wm. H. (HJ, K)

Jacobsen, -- (K)

Jacobsen, Gustave (TC)

Jacobsen, S. P. (E)

Jacobson, Gustav (H)

Jacokes, Daniel C. (R)

Jacokes, John Hood (R)

Jaeger, Adolph (H)

Jäger, Edmund (E)

Jäger, J. P. (K)

Jäger, Lehrer [teacher J. W. (GM)

Jahn, Friedrich Ludwig (G1, H)

Jahn, Julius (HJ)

Jahn-Heynsen, Frau -- (HJ)

Jahns, F. (T)

Jahns, H. C. T. (T)

Jahns, Wm. (T)

Jakowski, Augusta (A)

Jakowski, Minnie (A)

Jalatz, Henry B. (HJ)

Janauschek, Fanny (H)

Janke, Carl (SH)

Janke, Fritz (SH)

Janke, Marie (SH)

Janke, Sophie (SH)

Jans, Anneke (R)

Jansen, Petronella (SH)

Jansen, William (SH)

Janssen, Eduard (HJ)

Jantz, Harold (G2)

Jashinsky, Bertha (A)

Jashinsky, Charlotte (A)

Jashinsky, Fred (A)

Jashinsky, Frederick (A)

Jashinsky, Gottlieb (A)

Jashinsky, Gottlieb (A)

Jashinsky, Gustav (A)

Jashinsky, Julia (A)

Jashinsky, Martha (A)

Jastrow, Joseph (HJ)

Jauch, Carl J. (R)

Jebe, Susanne (G2)

Jegla, John J. (W)

Jelsch, Joseph (R)

Jenner, D. (T)

Jennings, Herbert Spencer (R)
Jensch, -- (TC)
Jensen, Georg (H)
Jentzsch, Dr. Ernest (TC)
Jevorutsky, Gust (A)
Jevorutsky, John (A)
Jörris, H. (K)
Johannes, Henry (R)
John, F. H. Rudolph (S)
Johnson, Hildegard Binder (G2)
Jones, Ferdinand (H)
Josenhans, Gottlieb (R)
Josephs, Joseph (R)
Jud, Johann Balthasar (S)
Judt, Friedrich C. (S)
Juergens, Dietrich (H, K)
Juergens, Emil (T)
Juergens, Paul (H)
Juessen, Edmund (H)
Juessen, Emil (HJ)
Julius, Frederick (SH)
Julius, Mary (SH)
Juncker/Yuncker, Jacob (W)
Juneau, S. (K)
Jung, Dr. -- (K)
Jung, Frank (R)
Jung, Johann (H, K)
Jung, Johann Christoph (S)
Jung, Ph. (T)
Jung, Wilhelm P. E. (S)
Jungk, Christian (E)
Jungman, -- (R)
Jungmann, Richard (HJ)

Kaas, Karl von (HJ)
Kadisch, L.J. (K)
Kaemmerling, -- (HJ)
Kaemper, Johann (H)
Kagey, Henry (R)
Kagi, John Henry (R)
Kahlenberg, Prof. -- (HJ)
Kahlfeld, William (SH)
Kahlfeld, Regina (SH)
Kahlman, Hermann (R)
Kahn, Albert (R)
Kahn, Julius (R)
Kahrmann, F. G. (E)
Kaichen, Arnold (R)
Kaiser, -- (R)
Kaiser, Eusebius (H)
Kaiser, J. (K)
Kaiser, R. A. (R)

Kainz, -- (HJ)

Kalb, Catherina (SH)

Kalb, Conrad (R)

Kalb, Ferdinand (SH)

Kalb, Joseph (HJ)

Kalbes, Mary (A)

Kalbus, Adam (A)

Kalbus, Augusta (A)

Kalbus (?), Charlotte (A)

Kalbus (?), Frieda (A)

Kalbus, Mollie (A)

Kalbus, William (A)

Kalckhoff, Dr. F. (K)

Kalckhoff, Gust. (K)

Kalkbronner, Wilhelm (R)

Kallenbach, -- (R)

Kalman, Ed. (T)

Kalt, Jos. P. (T)

Kalus, Anthony (R)

Kalvelage, H. (H)

Kalvelage, J. B. (T)

Kalzow, Fritz (R)

Kamerer, Charles (R)

Kaminski, Emily (A)

Kamp, Joseph B. (R)

Kamper, Louis (R)

Kampmeier, Wilhelm (S)

Kanause, John (R)

Kanause, William (R)

Kanitz, Louis (R)

Kanizer, N. (H)

Kannenberg, Lehrer [teacher] F. (GM)

Kannenkoth, Katharina (H)

Kanter, Edward (R)

Kanzler, Dr. Karl A. (R)

Kaple, John H. (R)

Kapp, Frederick (Friedrich) (H, HJ)

Kappler, Frederick C. (R)

Karbach, Philipp (S)

Karberg, Peter (E)

Karm, Adolph (H)

Karrer, Simon C. (R)

Kasper/Casper, Peter (W)

Kasselmann, C. J. (H)

Kassuba, C. L. W. (T)

Kassuba, H. W. (T)

Kast, Gustave (R)

Kasten, C. F. (K)

Kasten, Fred (T)

Kasten, Dr. Julius (T)

Kastler, Nikolaus (H)

Kater, Simon (E)

Katerbau, W. (H)

Kathmann, Henry (SH)

Katte, R. (K)

Katz, H. (K)

Katzer, --, Erzbischof (HJ)

Kauffer, Hale P. (R)

Kauffman, Calvin H. (R)

Kauffman, Louis G. (R)

Kauffman, Peter (R)

Kauffman, Samuel (R)

Kauffman, William (TC)

Kauffmann, Friedrich (S)

Kaufman, Fritz (R)

Kaufman, L. G. (R)

Kaufmann, H. (K)

Kaufmann, Wilhelm (H)

Kaun, Hugo (HJ)

Kauper, Geo. F. (T)

Kautz, -- (HJ)

Keck brothers (H)

Keeler, Henry (R)

Keider, John (R)

Keifer, E. W. (R)

Keiff, Lorenz (R)

Keil, C. F. (HJ)

Keilen, Christopher (W)

Keinester, -- (HJ)

Keiser, Christian (R)

Keiser, G. E. (T)

Keller, Dr. H. F. (R)

Keller, Henry (G1)

Keller, Isidor (HJ)

Keller, Pastor Otto Ph. (GM)

Kellinger, Father Louis (R)

Kellner, Charles Frederick (R)

Kellner, Michael (HJ)

Kellner, Wm. (T)

Kellog, L. S. (K)

Kellog, E. C. (K)

Kellog, W. A. (K)

Kelpe, Paul (H)

Kemp, Nicholas (R)

Kemper, H. G. (K)

Kemper, Hermann (HJ)

Kemper, John (W)

Kemper, Dr. K. (K)

Kemper, Louis (K)

Kemper, M. (T)

Kemper, Mrs. Philipp (H)

Kemper, Sebastian (R)

Kempf, Charles L. (R)

Kempf, Michael (R)
Kempfer, Rev. John F. (E)
Kempff, Nicholas (R)
Kempka, Alexander (A)
Kempka, Anna (A)
Kempka, Charles (A)
Kempka, Joseph (A)
Kempka (?), Mary (A)
Kempka, Mollie (A)
Kempke, Julius (A)
Kempke, Julius Charles (A)
Kempky, Pauline (A)
Kempky, Samuel (A)
Kencke, Fr. (K)
Kenkel, -- (TC)
Kenkel, F. P. (H)
Kenna, "Hinky Dink" (H)
Kennard, Joseph (H)
Kephart, Dr. Philip (R)
Keplius, -- (R)
Keppler, -- (HJ)
Kerich, Peter (H)
Kerkmann, Heinrich (HJ)
Kerkmann, John (HJ)
Kerl, Fritz (HJ)
Kerler, Eduard (F)
Kerler, Hermann (F)
Kerler, Johannes (F)
Kerler, Johannes, Jr. (F)
Kerler, Louis (F)
Kern, Carl Julius (HJ, K)
Kern, Heinrich (R)
Kern, J. B. A. (HJ)
Kern, John F. (HJ, T)
Kern, Rev. P. (E)
Kerner, Frederick W. (R)
Kerner, Otto (H)
Kernper, Joseph L. (R)
Kerschner, Andrew (R)
Kersler, Fred (R)
Kersten, Theo. (HJ)
Keshenberg, Augusta (A)
Keshenberg, Mina (A)
Keshenberg, William (A)
Kessler, Charles (H)
Kessler, Franz (H)
Kessler, W. S. (R)
Kettner, William (R)
Ketzler, F. (K)
Keusch, Lawrence (W)
Keyl, Pastor -- (K)
Kibbe, Alfred (HJ)

Kieckhefer, F. A. W. (HJ, T)
Kieckhefer, Wm. (HJ)
Kiefer, Albert (G1)
Kiefer, Carl (R)
Kiefer, Dr. Herman (R)
Kiel, Wm. (E)
Kierstede, Dr. Hans (R)
Kieselbach, Scott (G2)
Kies, -- (R)
Kiesling, August (SH)
Kiesling, Hanna (SH)
Kiesling, Herman (SH)
Kiesling, John (SH)
Kiesling, Rudolph (SH)
Kiesling, Sophie (SH)
Kiesser, J. B. (E)
Kiewert, Charles L. (HJ, T)
Kiewert, Emil (HJ)
Kiewert, Robert (HJ)
Kihlholz, B. (H)
Kilde, A.C. (HJ)
Kilian, Justus (H)
Killner, Max (R)
Kimbaldt, John H. (R)
Kimmel, Edward F. (R)
Kimmel, Henry (R)
Kindelberger, Jacob (R)
Kindemann, Charles (R)
Kindermann, Pastor -- (K)
Kindermann, -- (HJ)
Kindling, Louis (T)
Kindt, Louis (H, HJ)
Kineske, Hannah (R)
Kinipel, Henry Joseph (R)
Kinkel, Gottfried (H, HJ, K)
Kino, Father (Eusebius Kühn) (G2)
Kiolbassa, Peter (H)
Kipp, F. J. (T)
Kirch, Anna (SH)
Kirch, Nicolas (SH)
Kirchhoff, Chas. (T)
Kirchhoff, Mrs. H. A. (H)
Kirchhoff, Heinrich (S)
Kirchner, Adolph (R)
Kirchner, George H. (R)
Kirchner, Otto (R)
Kirchstein,Carl (SH)
Kirchstein, Caroline (SH)
Kirschmann, Christian (S)
Kissinger, John P. (HJ, T)
Kitzling, Dr. (K)
Klann, Jul. (T)

Klapproth, Hugo (G2)
Klar, Franz (H)
Klassek, Friedrich (W)
Klauer, Fred (HJ)
Klaussen, K. E. (S)
Klauser, Julius (HJ)
Klausmeyer, Emma (G2)
Klawater, Jacob (R)
Klebs, Edwin (H)
Kleffler, Dr. -- (K)
Klein, -- (HJ)
Klein, -- (R)
Klein, F. R. (HJ)
Klein, Hubert (W)
Klein, John (W)
Klein, Josef (H)
Klein, Julius (H)
Klein, M. J. (R)
Klein, Dr. Peter (R)
Klein, Samuel (R)
Klein, Theodore (W)
Kleine, Gustav Adolph (R)
Kleine, Dr. Lewis (R)
Kleinhaus, Michael (H)
Kleinknecht, Conrad (SH)
Kleis, Christian (E)
Klem, Stephen Vincent (R)
Klepetko, Frank (R)
Kletsch, Dr. G. U. (HJ)
Kletzsch, Dr. G. A (T)
Klett, Sophia (R)
Kletzsch, H. O. (T)
Klindworth, Karl (R)
Kling, Philip (R)
Klingbeil, Maria (SH)
Klinger, Nicholas (H)
Klingensmith, Frank L. (R)
Klinghammer, Crescens (SH)
Klinghammer, Nicolas (SH)
Klingholz, Chas. (HJ)
Klingholz, Richard (HJ)
Klingmann, William (H)
Klinker, John (E)
Kloberdanz, Timothy (G2)
Kloehn, Jul. H. (T)
Kloeckner, Anton (W)
Klokke, A.F. (H)
Klopp, -- (K)
Kloss, Martin (A)
Kloss, Peter (H)
Klügel, Pastor -- (K)
Klug, Otto (E)

Klumb, Phillip (E)

Kluppak, J. (K)

Knab, David (HJ, K)

Knaebel, Carl Henry (R)

Knapheide, Rudolph (G1, G2)

Knapp, J. G. (K)

Knapp, M. L. (H)

Knapper, Louis (R)

Knappstein, Heinrich (H)

Knauft, Ferdinand (G1)

Knauss, Jakob J. (S)

Knausas, Ludwig (S)

Kneeland, J. (K)

Kneeland, M. (K)

Knees, Wm. (SH)

Knell, Christoph (HJ)

Knieps/Knips, Nikolaus (W)

Knight, George Wells (R)

Knipschler, Father John E. (R)

Knobelsdorf, Ernst (H)

Knoll, F. M. (E)

Knoop, Henry (W)

Knopf, Oscar F. (TC)

Knopf, P. (H)

Knopp, Adam (H)

Knor, J. J. (HJ)

Knotser, E. A. (HJ)

Knotser, F. A. (HJ)

Knutson, Harold (G1)

Kobeler, Frederick (R)

Kobus, Augusta (A)

Kobus, Bertha (A)

Kobus, Emil (A)

Kobus, Emil J. (A)

Kobus, Hattie (A)

Kobus, John (A)

Kobus, John (A)

Kobus, Martha (A)

Kobus, Michael (A)

Kobus, Mollie (A)

Kobus, Mollie (A)

Kobus, Wilhelm (A)

Kobus, William (A)

Koch, Charles (H)

Koch, Kapt. Heinrich (E)

Koch, H. C. (HJ)

Koch, Herr. (R)

Koch, Ignatz (S)

Koch, J. C. (HJ)

Koch, John C. (T)

Koch, John F. (HJ)

Koch, O. (HJ)

Koch, Peter (R)

Koch, Robert (H)

Koch, Theodore W. (R)

Koch, W. (HJ)

Koch, W. C. L. (HJ)

Koch, William (R)

Kock, Pastor C. F. (GM)

Kocker, Peter (R)

Koczsky, Charlotte (A)

Köffler, C. A. (K)

Koeffler, Hugo (T)

Koenig, A. (T)

Koehler, Bernhard (H)

Koenig, C. A. (H)

Koehler, Frederick (R)

Koehler, Heinrich (E)

Köhler, Prof. J. (GM)

Koehler, Joseph (R)

Koehler, Robert (HJ)

Köhne, Karl (HJ)

Koelling, John (H)

Koenig, Rev. Charles J. (R)

Koenig, Conrad W. (R)

Koenig, George Augustus (R)

Koenig/King, Jacob (W)

Koenig, Selma S. (R)

Koenig, U. P. (T)

Koenig, William (R)

Koepfert/Goepferd/Gephart, Dominick (W)

Koeplinger, John (R)

Koeppen, Geo. (HJ)

Körner, -- (K)

Koerner, August (G1)

Koerner, Christ. (HJ)

Koerner, Fred (HJ)

Koerner, Gustav (H, HJ, TC)

Koester, Michael (R)

Koester, William (R)

Köwing, Johann Friedrich (S)

Kohl, -- (HJ)

Kohl, John George (R)

Kohler, -- (HJ)

Kohler, August (R)

Kohler, Kaufman (R)

Kohler, Max James (R)

Kohlhans, -- (HJ)

Kohlmann, B. (K)

Kohlsaat, Hermann (H)

Kohn, -- (K)

Kohne, Prof. Christopher J. (R)

Kokenge, Prof. John B. (R)

Kolp, Nickolas (W)

Kompe, Frederick W. (SH)

Kompl, Henry (SH)

Konietzke, William (A)

Konstanski, Wilhelm (A)

Konti, Isadore (R)

Kooven, Dr. -- (K)

Kopatz, Bertha (A)

Kopatz, Mollie (A)

Kopf, -- (K)

Kopf, Johannes M. (S)

Kopitz, Adolph D. (SH)

Kopke, August (SH)

Kopke, Augusta (SH)

Kopke, Henriette (SH)

Kopmeier, J. H. (T)

Kopp, -- (K)

Kopp, Rev. -- (R)

Kopp, Anthony (R)

Kopp, Jacob (H)

Kopp, William (H)

Korfliage, A. (H)

Korn, Wm. H. (E)

Korte, Peter (R)

Kosel/Cosel, Frank (W)

Koss, Charles (T)

Kossak, Dr. J. (K)

Kost, Dr. John (R)

Koster, -- (R)

Koster, John (W)

Kostreva, Fred (A)

Kostreva, Fred (A)

Kostreva, Gottlieb (A)

Kostreva, Gottlieb (A)

Kostreva, Gottlieb (A)

Kostreva, John (A)

Kostreva, John (A)

Kostreva, John (A)

Kostreva, John (A)

Kostreva, Julia (A)

Kostreva (?), Laura (A)

Kostreva, Minnie (A)

Kostreva, Minnie (A)

Kostreva, Ruth (A)

Kostreva, Samuel (A)

Kostreva, William (A)

Kotz, Charles (H)

Kotz, Rudolph (HJ)

Kovalski, Michael (A)

Kovalski, Wilhelmina (A)

Kovatz, August (H)

Kovatz, Dr. E. (T)

Kovneski, Frederick (A)

Kovnesky, John (A)

Kovnesky, Michael (A)

Kowalski, Caroline (A)

Kraatz, Frau Chas. (T)

Kraatz, E. (K)

Kraetsch, Paul J. (E)

Kraft, Joseph (H)

Krage, M. (H)

Krahmer, Edward (SH)

Krahmer, Philomena (SH)

Krahn, H. (K)

Krak, Dr. -- (K)

Krake, Rev. Blasius (R)

Kramer, August (H)

Kramer, J. P. (H)

Kramer/Krammer, John (W)

Kramer, Joseph (W)

Kramer, Mathias (W)

Krampe, Louis (H)

Kranich, Edward F. (R)

Krantz, -- (K)

Krapf, Conrad (R)

Krapp, Conrad (R)

Krasta, Caroline (A)

Kratz, Leonard (R)

Kratz, Mary (R)

Kraus, Berthold (E)

Kraus, Edward H. (R)

Kraus, Ezra Jacob (R)

Kraus, Fred (T)

Kraus, Konrad (S)

Kraus, Theodor (S)

Krause, --, Pastor (HJ, K)

Krause, Adam (A)

Krause, Benj. H. (R)

Krause, Caroline (A)

Krause, Charles (A)

Krause, Erdinthe (SH)

Krause, Ferdinand (SH)

Krause, Gustav (A)

Krause, Henry (R)

Krause, Michael (A)

Krause, Minnie (A)

Krause, Minnie (A)

Krause, Robert (E)

Krause, Samuel (A)

Krause, Samuel (A)

Krause, Samuel (A)

Krause, Wilhelm (A)

Krause, William (A)

Kraut, Franz (SH)

Krautbauer, --, Bischof (HJ)

Krebs, E. W. (T)

Krecke, Florenz (R)

Kregger, Michael (R)

Krehbiel, Christian (S)

Krehbiel, Henry Edward (R)

Kreischer, Joseph Henry (R)

Kreiser, Michael (H)

Krejci, Dr. J. C. (E)

Krekeler, Anthony (W)

Krekeler, Heinz (H)

Krembs, Ernst (HJ)

Kremer, Conrad J. (R)

Kremer, Gerhard (G2)

Kremer, John (HJ, T)

Kremer, John (R)

Kremer, Prof. John B. (R)

Kremers, Prof. -- (HJ)

Kremke, Wilhelm (R)

Krenerich, Peter (R)

Krentel, Andrew Peter (R)

Krentkampf, Rev. Ferdinand (R)

Kresge, Sebastian (R)

Kretlow, Ed. (HJ)

Kretz, A. (K)

Kretschmer, Khas. G. (E)

Kreuter, -- (K)

Kreutzer, Andrew (HJ)

Krez, Konrad (HJ)

Krezer, John M. (R)

Kriege, Hermann (H, TC)

Krieglstein, William (H)

Krier, Mathias (H)

Krieter, Friedrich (H)

Krinbill, Andrew (H)

Krinbill, Georg (H)

Kroeger, Arnold (H)

Kroeger, Hermann (HJ, K)

Kroehuke, -- (HJ)

Krönke, Diedrich (S)

Krönlein, Johann Michael (S)

Kromberger, Hans (G2)

Krommer, Prof. A. J. (E)

Kron, Karl (HJ)

Kronenwetter, S. (HJ)

Kronshage, Theodor (HJ)

Kropf, O. A. (T)

Kropf, Oscar F. (TC)

Krouskop, -- (HJ)

Krueger, -- (HJ)

Kruer, August (HJ)

Krüger, Fischer (HJ)

Krüger, F. (K)

Krüer, A. (K)

Kruetgen, Ernest (H)

Krüppel, G. (HJ)

Krug, -- (K)

Krug, A. (K)

Krug, August (HJ)

Krull, Robt. (T)

Krumwiede, Charles (G2)

Kruse, Friedrich (H)

Kruse, Michael (S)

Kruse, William F. (TC)

Kruse, William (H)

Kryzanowski, Wladimir (HJ)

Kryzkawa, -- (K)

Kuehn, A. M. (T)

Kuehn, Ferdinand (HJ, K, T)

Kuehn, Jul. (T)

Kuehn, Otto (T)

Kuehns, Carl (HJ)

Kuenzli, Henry (T)

Küpper, Chs. (K)

Kuestermann, Gustav (HJ)

Kuh, Edwin (H)

Kuhl, J. (H)

Kuhl, Maria (SH)

Kuhl, Mathias (SH)

Kuhlemeyer, A. H. (E)

Kuhlenhölter, Simon (S)

Kuhn, Pastor A., Sr. (GM)

Kuhn, Christian (H)

Kuhn, Fritz (H)

Kuhn , Pastor G. A. (GM)

Kuhn, John (H)

Kuhnen, N. (E)

Kulas, Father John (G2)

Kull, -- (HJ)

Kuman, Christian (SH)

Kuman, Louisa (SH)

Kummel, Gertrude (SH)

Kummel, Joseph, Sr. (SH)

Kundig, Martin (HJ, K)

Kundinger, Sig. (T)

Kunitzki, John (HJ)

Kunkelmann/Kunzelmann, Adam (W)

Kuntz, Louis (H)

Kupachky, Maria (A)

Kupper, Paul F. (HJ)

Kupshehova, Mary (A)

Kurits, Bill (H)

Kurz, Frank (H)

Kurz, Hedwig (HJ, K)

Kurz, H. (K)

Kurz, Heinrich (HJ, K)

Kurz, Joseph (HJ, K)

Kurz, Julius (H)

Kurz, Louis (H, HJ, K)

Kurz, Pepi (HJ, K)

Kurz, Peter (T)

Kurztisch, Herm. (T)

Kuss, Richard (H)

Kussman, Ernest G. (TC)

Kusswurm, E. (H)

Kuter, Israel (H)

Kutrib, Carolin (A)

LaBusch, Katherine (A)

Lachmund, -- (HJ)

Lackner, -- (K)

Lackner, Anton (K)

Lackner, F. C. (K)

Lackner, Franz (HJ, K)

Lafrentz, Ferdinand (H)

Lahrmann, B. H. (E)

Laiboldt, -- (HJ)

Lambach, Heinrich (E)

Lambert, D. (K)

Lambert, Peter (E)

Lampmann, Heinrich (H)

Lampmann, J. (H)

Landauer, Ad. (T)

Landauer, Mar. (HJ)

Landeck, G. J. (T)

Landgraff, -- (K)

Landmeyer, G. (H)

Landvatter, M. (K)

Landwehr, H. (H)

Lang, C. (K)

Lang, Thomas (H)

Lange, A. (S)

Lange, Chas. (T)

Lange, G. M. (K)

Lange, L. A. (T)

Lange, Paul (E)

Langguth, Christian (H)

LaSalle, Jacob (H)

Lasche, Ernst (HJ)

Lassig, Moritz (H)

Laubenheimer, J. J. (K)

Lauderbach, Michael (SH)

Lauderbach, Susanna (SH)

Lauer, -- (K)

Lauer, Carl (SH)

Lauer, Catharina (SH)

Lauer, Charles (SH)

Lauer, Kaspar (H)

Laufer, Berthold (H)

Laugheinrich, Gottfried (H)

Laux, M. (H)

Laverrenz, O. (K)

Lavis, -- (K)

Lederer, Johann (G2)

Lefens, Thies (H)

Legler, Fridolin, Jr. (HJ)

Legler, Fridolin, Sr. (HJ)

Legler, George (HJ)

Legler, Henry (H, HJ)

Legler, H. E. (HJ)

Legler, J. Kaspar (HJ)

Lehmann, -- (HJ, K)

Lehmann, Augusta (H)

Lehmann, Ernst J. (H)

Lehmann, John (W)

Lehner, John (E)

Lehrer, Anna (SH)

Lehrer, Michael (SH)

Lehrkind, F. (K)

Leibhold, P. F. (SH)

Leibhold, Sybilla (SH)

Leidel, C. R. M. (HJ)

Leidersdorf, B. (T)

Leik, Henry (W)

Leik, Paul (W)

Leisch, W. C. (HJ)

Leisner, Caroline (A)

Leisner, Wilhelm (A)

Leitshul, Elisa (SH)

Leitshul, Thomas (SH)

Lembcke, -- (K)

Lemcke, Heinrich (H)

Leminger, Martin (SH)

Leminger, Theresia (SH)

Lender, Robert (H)

Lennemann/Lenneman, Franz (W)

Lenschau, Ferdinand (S)

Lentz (?), Catalina (A)

Lentz, Gottlieb (A)

Lentz, Gustav (A)

Lentz, Gustav (A)

Lentz (?), Katherine (A)

Lentz, Michael (A)

Lentz, Steve (A)

Lenz, John (HJ)

Lerch, Wm. (E)

Lesemann, Karoline (H)

Lessenick, John J. (E)

Lester, Henry C. (G2)

Letz, Jacob (H)

Leuthold, Heinrich (HJ)

Leutze, Emmanuel (HJ)

Leuw, Dr. L. de (K)

Lewantowska, Selma (K)

Leyschmidt, A. (HJ)

Lieb, Hermann (H)

Lieber, Francis (H)

Lieber, Franz (HJ)

Lieber, H. (HJ, K)

Lieber, Peter (SH)

Lieber, Sophie (SH)

Lieberthal, David (H)

Liebig, Justus von (HJ)

Liebhaber, J. A. (HJ, K)

Lienhardt, A. (K)

Liermann, Hermann (H)

Liese, S. (S)

Liginger, J. B. (K)

Lill, William (H)

Lindblom, Robt. (HJ)

Linde, J. (HJ)

Lindemann, -- (HJ)

Lindemann, Karoline (H)

Linden, M. (K)

Lindwurm, M. (K)

Lingg, Louis (H, TC)

Lingsch, Emil (T)

Linke, F. Oscar (HJ)

Lipp, Anna Maria (SH)

Lipp, Ulrich (SH)

Lippert, Robert (H)

Lippich, Angelo (H)

Lischer, Henry (E)

Lischer, Julius (E)

Litsinger, Edward (H)

Lob, Otto (H)

Lobbecke, Friedrich (H)

Locher, Catharina (SH)

Locher, John (SH)

Lochner, Pastor -- (K)

Loeb, Adolph (H)

Loebel, Paul (H)

Löber, H. (T)

Löffelholz, A. (T)

Löffler, Oscar (T)

Löher, Franz (Gl, HJ)

Loeher, Prof. Franz X. (W)

Loeher, Paul (HJ)

Loesch, Frank J. (TC)

Loewe, Hermann (H)

Löwenbach, H. (T)

Loewenthal, Bernhard (H)

Logauer, Dr. -- (K)

Logemann, Georg (HJ)

Logemann, Geo., Jr. (T)

Lohe, H. (HJ)

Loheide, Christina Y. (SH)

Loheide, Henry G. (SH)

Lohmiller, Ludwig (H)

Lohn, Christian (H)

Longeley, John (HJ)

Longenecker, J.M. (H)

Loose, Heinrich (HJ, K)

Lorenz, Arthur (H)

Lorenz, Pastor Paul (GM)

Lorenz, Richard (HJ)

Lorenzen, C. (K)

Lorenzen, Th. (K)

Loth, G. (K)

Loth, "Papa" (HJ)

Lotz, Louis (T)

Lowitz, Lehrer [teacher] F. (GM)

Louis, H. E. (HJ)

Lubbers, Paul (E)

Luchfinger, John (HJ)

Luckenbach, Anton (W)

Ludloff, Karl (HJ)

Ludvigh, Samuel (G2, K)

Ludwig, Agnes (H)

Ludwig, H. (K)

Ludwig, John C. (HJ)

Ludwig, William R. (H)

Lüddemann, A. (K)

Lueder, August (TC)

Lueder, Arthur (H)

Lüder, C. H. (K)

Lueders, August (H)

Luedke, H. August (HJ, T)

Lüning, Dr. -- (K)

Lüning, A., Jr. (K)

Luening, A. F. (HJ)

Luening, Eugen (HJ)

Luening, Eugene (T)

Luening, Dr. F. A. (HJ)

Lüning, W. (K)

Lüers, -- (K)

Lüps, Jacob (HJ)

Lufft, C. (HJ)

Lufsky, Julius (T)

Lumbard, Franz (H)

Lungerhausen, Traugott (R)

Lusch, A. I. (E)

Luthardt, John N. (R)

Luther, Henry (HJ, K)
Lutterbeck, Eugen (H)
Luttig/Luettich, William (W)
Lutz, Rev. Fred (HJ)
Lutz, Dr. Frederick (R)
Lutze, B. C. (E)
Lutze, J. J. (R)
Lymburner, Adam (R)
Lynde, Chr. J. (K)
Lynde, W. P. (HJ, K)
Lysek, Augusta (A)
Lyser, Gustav (HJ)

Maas, Aug. (HJ)
Maas, Hubert (H)
Maas, John B. (R)
Mack, -- (R)
Mack, Christian (R)
Mack, Edwin F. (R)
Mack, Louis (K)
Mack, Mary (SH)
Mack, Peter (SH)
Madding, L.B. (HJ)
Maderfield, Nicholas Hubert (R)
Maentz, Henry (R)
Märker, Alex. (T)
Märker, H. C. (T)
Maerker, Wilhelm (H)
Märklin, Edmund (HJ, K)
Mager, John (H)
Magius, -- (K)
Magnus, Christian (E)
Magnus, Conrad (SH)
Magnus, Dorothea (SH)
Magnus, Lenora (SH)
Magnus, Paul (SH)
Maher, Georg (H)
Mahler, Emma (HJ, K)
Mahler, Jacob (HJ, K)
Mahler, J. F. (H)
Mahr, Wm. (HJ)
Mahraun, H. (E)
Maibaum, H. (K)
Maier, Martin (R)
Mainhan, Eugene (R)
Maissen, Thomas (W)
Maiwurm/Meiwurm, John (W)
Maladon, John (R)
Malmros, Oscar (HJ)
Maltz, George L. (R)
Malzacher, Louis (H, TC)
Malzacher, M. (H)

Mand, John A. (T)

Mandel, E. (H)

Mandel, Leon (H)

Manderfelt, Anton (SH)

Manderfelt, Cecilia (SH)

Manderfelt, Clara (SH)

Manderfelt, Hubert (SH)

Manderfelt, John (SH)

Manderfelt, Maria (SH)

Manderfelt, Peter (SH)

Manderfelt, Susanna (SH)

Mandernheid, John (E)

Manderscheid, John (T)

Mandorff, Rachel (R)

Manegold, Chas. (T)

Manegold, Chas., Jr. (HJ)

Mangerich, Michael (W)

Mangold, F. X. (E)

Manisur, Georg (H)

Mann, Chas. L. (T)

Mann, G. M. (T)

Mann, Gother (R)

Mann, Henry (HJ, T)

Mann, Henry (R)

Mann, J. E. (T)

Mann, John (H)

Mann, Lena A. (T)

Mann, Otto L. (H)

Mann, Peter (R)

Mann, Walter (G2)

Mannhardt, Emil (H)

Mannheimer, Michael (H)

Manning, Daniel (W)

Manz, Jacob (H)

Marbach, Joseph (H, TC)

Margenau, Roy Edward (R)

Margenruth, Dora (R)

Marheinecke, -- (HJ)

Mario, Rev. Matthias M. (R)

Mark, Rt. Rev. Ignatius (R)

Mark, John (R)

Mark, John (R)

Marks, Christiane (G2)

Marks, M. (T)

Marling, Geo. (HJ)

Marling, G. W. (T)

Marnitz, Wm. (T)

Marr, Carl (HJ)

Marschall, Rosanna (H)

Marschner, Adolph F. (R)

Marschner, Alfred (HJ)

Martens, August Detlef (E)

Marth, -- (R)

Martin, Anton (W)

Martin, Anton (W)

Martin, Conrad (W)

Martin, Conrad (W)

Martin, Franz (W)

Martin, George (HJ)

Martin, Geo., Jr. (T)

Martin, John Joseph (W)

Martin, Joseph (W)

Martin, Nikolaus (W)

Martin, Peter (H)

Martini, G. (T)

Martini, Joseph (H)

Martz, Frank (R)

Martz, Michael (R)

Marx, Marcus (H)

Marx, Mathias (H)

Marx, Stephen (R)

Marxhausen, August (R)

Maschauer, Lorenz (HJ, T)

Massaquoi, Hans (H)

Massbacher, Franz (R)

Massenberg, Wilhelm (H)

Massman, John C. (G2)

Mast, A. F. (E)

Mast, Prof. S. O. (R)

Mast, Samuel Ottomar (R)

Matenaers, F. (H)

Mathei, Philip (H)

Mathes, Christian (E)

Mathes, E. (H)

Mathes, H. (HJ)

Mathies, Gen. C. (E)

Matt, Joseph (G2)

Mattern, Friedrich (H, TC)

Mattern, Lorenz (H)

Mattes, John Jr. (E)

Mattes, Paul (E)

Matthai, -- (R)

Matthaus, Adam (R)

Matthey, Dr. Carl (E)

Matthey, H. Sr. (E)

Matthey, Heinrich (E)

Matthieson, A. (K)

Mattrisch, Adolph (A)

Mattrisch, Gottlieb (A)

Mattrisch, William (A)

Mattrisch, William (A)

Matullath, Hugo (R)

Matz (Mix), Adolph (A)

Matz, Otto (H)

Mauch, Max (H)

Mauch, Bernard (R)

Mauch, Joseph William (R)

Mauer, John Peter (W)

Mauer, Philip (R)

Mauff, August (H)

Maul, Georg (S)

Maus, Jacob (R)

Mauthe, C. (E)

Maurin, Marcus (G2)

May, Barbara (SH)

May, Christian (SH)

Mayer, Augustin K. (R)

Mayer, Charles F. (HJ)

Mayer, Joseph (H)

Mayer, Leo (H)

Mayer, Levy (H, TC)

Mayer, Louis (HJ)

Mayer, Oscar (H, TC)

Mayer, Theo. P. (HJ)

Maxis, Terese (R)

Medill, Joseph (H)

Meding, A. (K)

Meessmann, Dr. Hugo (T)

Mehrmann, -- (K)

Meier, Henry (R)

Meier, J. J. (HJ, K)

Meigs, Montgomery (R)

Meile, Fred (SH)

Meile, Margaret (SH)

Meili, Hans H. (S)

Meincke, Bruno (R)

Meinecke, Adolph (HJ, T)

Meinecke, Fred (T)

Meiners, Gerhard (H)

Meiners, Rev. Herman (R)

Meiners, J. (K)

Meininger, John (H)

Meinken, Lehrer [teacher] A.C.F. (GM)

Meinzer, -- (K)

Meisneft, Dr. -- (HJ)

Meinz, George J. (G2)

Meissner, F. W. (T)

Meiszner, John (H)

Meister, J. (K)

Meitzner, E. A. (HJ)

Melcher, Jos. (HJ)

Melchers, Carl (R)

Melchers, Julius Theodore (R)

Melms, Alb. (HJ, K)

Melms, G. T. (HJ)

Mels, A. (H)

Meltzer, Carl (TC)

Meltzler, William Douglas (R)

Melzer, John (SH)

Melzer, Mina (SH)

Memminger, J. (K)

Menche, Alfred Herman (R)

Mende, Erich (H)

Mendel, H. M. (HJ, T)

Mendelsohn, Albert (R)

Mendelson, Louis (R)

Mengelberg, Rud. (T)

Mengelhauer, Frank (H)

Mengert, Johannes (S)

Menn, Rudolf (H)

Menninger, William (R)

Mensel, Ernest Heinrich (R)

Menter John W. (R)

Mentis, Johann (HJ)

Menz, John (E)

Menzel, -- (K)

Merendorff, S. Joseph (R)

Merian, Kasper (R)

Merker, Heinrich (H)

Merkle, George (SH)

Merkle, Heinrich (H)

Merkle, Veronica (SH)

Mernitz, Joachim F. (S)

Merz, -- (K)

Merz, Leonhard (HJ)

Mesemer, Anton (SH)

Mesemer, Anton (SH)

Mesemer, Joseph (SH)

Mesemer, Mary (SH)

Messenger, J. A. (K)

Messersmith, George (R)

Metle, August (R)

Metz, -- (R)

Metz, Christian (H)

Metz, Georg (H)

Metzen, -- (HJ)

Metzen, John (H)

Metzger, Pastor D. (GM)

Metzger, George (E)

Metzger, William A. (R)

Metzler, Philip (R)

Metzmer, --, Bischof (HJ)

Meuffels, Joseph (R)

Meunier, John (T)

Meusch, Philipp (S)

Meyenschein, Friedrich (H)

Meyer, Prof. -- (HJ, R)

Meyer, Ad. H. (HJ, T)

Meyer, Anna (SH)

Meyer, Antonia (SH)

Meyer, Augustine K. (R)

Meyer, C. J. L. (R)

Meyer, Carl (E)

Meyer, Casp. (K)

Meyer, Chas. G. (T)

Meyer, Dr. Chr. (K)

Meyer, C. H. (K)

Meyer, Charles (H)

Meyer, Charlotte (K)

Meyer, Ed. (HJ)

Meyer, Lt. Elias (R)

Meyer, Enno (K)

Meyer, Geo. (HJ)

Meyer, Geo. P. (T)

Meyer, H. A. (HJ)

Meyer, Pastor H. E. (GM)

Meyer, Henry (G2)

Meyer, J. (K)

Meyer, Johann (H)

Meyer, John (SH)

Meyer, John Jacob (R)

Meyer, Joseph (HJ)

Meyer, Mathias (H, TC)

Meyer, Matthew (SH)

Meyer, William (H)

Meyerding, Henry J. (SH)

Meyerding, Maria (SH)

Meyers, F. J. (T)

Meyers, Frederick (R)

Meyers, Henry (R)

Meyers, Jesse Jeremiah (R)

Meyers, Joseph (R)

Meyers, Joseph (W)

Meyers, Mathias (W)

Meyers, Michael (R)

Meyers, William J. (R)

Meyrose, --, Schmied (HJ, K)

Michael, George (SH)

Michael, Louis (R)

Michael, Mary (SH)

Michael, William (R)

Michaelis, Charles (SH)

Michaelis, Clara (TC)

Michaelis, Maria (SH)

Michaelis, Richard (H, TC)

Michaels, Pastor M.C. (GM)

Michalowski, Herm. (HJ)

Michel, -- (R)

Michel, C. (H)

Michel, John (R)

Michels, Ivan C. (HJ)
Michelson, Albert (H)
Middledorf, Ulrich (H)
Mieding, A. E. (T)
Mieding, Dr. (HJ)
Miege, Rt. Rev. J. B. (R)
Miesel, -- (R)
Miessler, Ernst (H)
Miguly, Rudolph (H)
Mihalotzy, -- (HJ)
Milbrath, Georg (HJ)
Milde, -- (HJ)
Millemann, Jacob (H)
Miller, Adam (W)
Miller, Albert (R)
Miller, Andreas (H)
Miller, Anton (W)
Miller, Fred (HJ)
Miller, Frederick (R)
Miller, Geo. P. (T)
Miller, Gertrude (W)
Miller, H. (HJ)
Miller, Henry (R)
Miller, Henry (R)
Miller, Henry B. (R)
Miller, Hubert (W)
Miller, Jacob (H)
Miller, Jacob (W)
Miller, John (W)
Miller, John (W)
Miller, John (R)
Miller, John Andrew (W)
Miller, John Michael (W)
Miller, John Peter (W)
Miller, John Peter (R)
Miller, Josef (H)
Miller, Mary (SH)
Miller, Mathias (H)
Miller, Mathias (W)
Miller, Mathias (SH)
Miller, Paul (SH)
Miller, Peter (W)
Miller, Peter (R)
Millins, Anton (R)
Minnuet, Peter (R)
Minwegen, Mathias (W)
Minwegen, Thomas (H)
Miokowski, -- (HJ)
Mitchell, John L. (T)
Mittelberger, Gottlieb (R)
Mock, B. (K)
Mock, L. (T)

Moehling, -- (R)

Moehlman, Arthur B. (R)

Moeller, Carl (SH)

Möller, Friedrich (H)

Moeller, Father Henry (R)

Moeller, Mina (SH)

Möllmann, -- (HJ)

Moersch, Julius (G1)

Mönstedt, A. (T)

Moffat, B. (K)

Mogk, George F. (R)

Mohme, H. J. (E)

Mohn, Harrison B. (R)

Mohr, Christian Albert (S)

Mohr, Henrietta (SH)

Mohr, John (SH)

Mohr, Jul. (K)

Mohr, Oscar (HJ, T)

Moldenhenker, Dr. Richard Gottlieb (R)

Molitor, David Albert (R)

Molitor, Edward (R)

Moll, Herman (R)

Mondschein, S. A. (T)

Monnig, Anthony (R)

Moorman, Fr. Otto J. (R)

Morell, George (R)

Moring, Frederick (R)

Moos, Bernhard (H)

Morawetz, Jacob (HJ, K)

Morawetz, M. L. (T)

Morgenschein, W. (K)

Morgenthau, Hans (H)

Moses, Adolph (H)

Moses, Dr. J. L. (HJ)

Mosdzen, Caroline (A)

Mosdzen, Jennie (A)

Mosdzen, Louise (A)

Moskowitt, Fr. (K)

Most, Johann (TC)

Mott, August (H)

Much, Karl (H)

Muchike, Friedrich (H)

Muehlhäuser, Pastor -- (HJ, K)

Mueller, -- (TC)

Müller, A. F. (K)

Müller, Andreas (S)

Mueller, Adolph (H)

Mueller, Alexander (HJ)

Müller, C. Jos. (T)

Mueller, Christian (H)

Müller, Christ. (E)

Müller, Ernst (E)

Mueller, Frederich (R)
Mueller, Friedrich (HJ)
Mueller, Prof. G. B. (HJ)
Müller, Gottlieb (S)
Mueller, Gustav (R)
Müller, H. (K)
Mueller, H. (R)
Mueller, Hermann (H)
Mueller, Jacob (H)
Müller, Johann (G2)
Mueller, John B. (R)
Mueller, Joseph (H)
Mueller, Louis F. (HJ)
Mueller, Mathias (H)
Mueller, Max (H)
Müller, Oscar A. (T)
Mueller, P. F. (HJ)
Mueller, Paul (H, TC)
Mueller, Peter (W)
Mueller, Robert (HJ)
Muench, Friedrich (HJ)
Muensterberg, Prof. Hugo (HJ)
Muenzberg, Paul (HJ)
Münzenmeyer, Aug. (E)
Münzer, Hieronymous (G2)
Müsing, Lehrer [teacher] (GM)
Muhlenberg, Heinrich (R)
Muhlmann, A. (H)
Muhs, Fred (SH)
Muhs, John (SH)
Muhs, Lena (SH)
Mulfinger, G. F. (H)
Mulithner, John Balthasar (R)
Muller, Bernard (R)
Muller, Catherine (SH)
Muller, Ida (SH)
Muller, Jacob (SH)
Muller, John (SH)
Muma, Fred (R)
Munch, Emil (G1)
Mundelein, Archbishop -- (TC)
Mundelein, George W. (H)
Mundt, Amelia (A)
Munk, Dr. -- (K)
Munk, Frln. [Ms.] -- (K)
Munk, --, Jr. (K)
Munkwitz, Chs. (K, T)
Muntsch, Prof. Albert (R)
Murer, John (E)
Murock, Ludwig (A)
Murrach, Caroline (A)
Murrach, Ida (A)

Murrach, Mary (A)

Murrach, Molly (A)

Murrach, William, Jr. (A)

Murrach, William, Sr. (A)

Mursau, Carl (A)

Mursau, Frederick (A)

Mursau, John (A)

Mursau, Ludwig (A)

Mursau, Michael (A)

Mursau, Pauline (A)

Myer, Frank B. (R)

Nägele, Lambert (G2)

Naft, Wilhelm (HJ)

Nagel, Dr. -- (K)

Nagel, Andrew (R)

Nagel, August (SH)

Nagel, Catharina (SH)

Nagel, Charles (H)

Nagel, F. (HJ)

Nagel, Lambert (SH)

Nagel, Liberata (SH)

Nahler, J. J. (TC)

Naprstek, B. (K)

Nasemann, Lorenz (W)

Nasgovitz, August (A)

Nasgovitz, Caroline (A)

Nasgovitz, Caroline (A)

Nasgovitz, Karl (A)

Nasgovitz, Ludwig (A)

Nasgovitz, Louise (A)

Nasgovitz, Wilhelmina (A)

Nasgovitz, William (A)

Natz, Frln. [Ms.] -- (K)

Nau, Constantine (W)

Naumann, Pastor J.H. (GM)

Nazro, J. (K)

Neberfeldt, William (R)

Neebe, Oscar (H, TC)

Neff, -- (R)

Neff, Ludwig (W)

Neumann, Jacob (W)

Nehrling, Heinrich [Henry] (HJ, T)

Neimann, D. (K)

Neshek, Albert (A)

Neshek, August (A)

Neshek, Augusta (A)

Neshek, Emil W. (A)

Neshek, Fred (A)

Neshek, John (A)

Neshek, Michael (A)

Nestel, Karl C. (S)

Netsorg, Bendetson (R)

Netter, John (R)

Neubert, Anton (H)

Neuchterlein, H. G. (R)

Neudorf, Nikolaus (H)

Neuer, J. B. (K)

Neuhaus, H. (K)

Neukirch, Chas. (HJ)

Neukirch, Franz (HJ)

Neukirch, C. (K)

Neukirch, F. (K)

Neuman, Wm. F. V. (R)

Neuman, Julia (R)

Neumann, C. (H, K)

Neumeyer, Jacob (E)

Neussel, William (H)

Neustad[e]l, J. (HJ, K)

Neustadel, Simon (HJ)

Newbouer, -- (K)

Newe, -- (K)

Newman, Charles (SH)

Newman, Emma (SH)

Neymann, Ad. (K)

Neymann, Emil (K)

Nichar, George H. (R)

Nichols, Anna (A)

Nickel, -- (K)

Niebuhr, Otto (H)

Niedecken, Chas. (T)

Niedecken, Ed. (T)

Niedecken, H. (HJ, K)

Niedecken, Henry (T)

Niedermann, H. (HJ, K)

Niedermeyer, Aug. (T)

Niemann-Rabe, -- (HJ)

Niemeier, G. (T)

Niemeyer, Chr. (K)

Niemeyer, Otto (HJ)

Nies, Konrad (H)

Nieschang, Dr. -- (K)

Niethammer, Otto (S)

Nimsz, Johan (SH)

Nimsz, Wilhelmina (SH)

Niswander, Frank J. (R)

Nitz, Charles (HJ)

Nitze, William (H)

Nitzschke, E. (K)

Nix, Jacob (G2)

Nix, Jacob (SH)

Nix, Margaretta (SH)

Nix, Peter (SH)

Nockemann, W. (K)

Noecker, John (R)
Noehren, Rev. H. (HJ)
Noeker, Franz (W)
Nölting, F. L. (K)
Noete, John (R)
Nöthig, Dr. -- (K)
Noll, Conrad (R)
Nollau, Louis E. (S)
Nolle, Franz (SH)
Nolte, H. A. (T)
Noot, William (G1)
Nott, Rev. H. C. (HJ)
Notz, Dr. W. (HJ)
Novy, Frederick G. (R)
Nuffer, Frederick (R)
Nunnemacher, Emilie (T)
Nunnemacher, H. (K)
Nunnemacher, J. (K)
Nunnemacher, Rob. (T)
Nurenberg, Joseph (W)
Nussbaum, Rt. Rev. Paul J. (R)
Nusser, John (HJ)

Obenauer, Marie Louise (R)
Oberdorffer, William J. (R)
Oberhart, A. (H)
Obermann, Geo. (HJ)
Obermann, Jacob (HJ)
Oberndorfer, Henry M. (T)
Obetz, Henry L. (R)
Ochne, T. (H)
Ochs, Anton (SH)
Ochs, Francis (E)
Ochs, Walburga (SH)
Ochsenhert, Adam (R)
Odell, Anton (R)
Odren, Alexander (R)
Ody, -- (K)
Ody, J. (K)
Oehle, Gottfired (HJ)
Oehm, -- (K)
Oehm, Catharina (K)
Oertel, Maximilian (HJ)
Oesan, -- (HJ)
Oestreicher, John (T)
Oether, Joseph (SH)
Oether, Mary Ann (SH)
Oettinger, -- (K)
Off, Karl F. (S)
Ohlinger, Gustavus (TC)
Ohm, R. (H)
Oldenburg, Chas. (HJ)

Ollech, John (A)

Ollech, Wilhelmina (A)

Olsen, Esther (H)

Olshefski, Frank (A)

Olshefski, Fred (A)

Olshefski, Michael (A)

Olshetski, Bertha (A)

Opitz, H. (HJ, K)

Oppen, Heinrich von (H)

Orban, F. W. (K)

Orendorf, A. (HJ)

Orendorff, -- (K)

Orff, Henry (HJ, K)

Orschel, Marina (H)

Ortelius, Abraham (G2)

Orth, -- (R)

Orth, Adam (HJ)

Orth, Chas. A. (T)

Orth, Ph. (T)

Orthwein, Friderich (G2)

Ortman, Charles L. (R)

Ortseifen, Adam (H)

Ortwein, Friedrich (G1)

Osius, George (R)

Ossendorf,Kurt (H)

Ostenfeld, Wm. (HJ)

Osterhaus, -- (HJ)

Ostlangemberg, O.G. (H)

Ostrander, W. (HJ)

Oswald, Dr. -- (K)

Oswald, A. (HJ)

Oswald, Leonhard (SH)

Oswald, Martin (HJ)

Oswald, Sabina (SH)

Otgen, Christian (R)

Otgen, Theobald (R)

Otjen, Theobald (HJ)

Ott, Christian (HJ, K)

Ott, Emil H. (T)

Ott, Jacob (H)

Ott, Mathias (W)

Otten, Prof. John (R)

Ottendorfer, Anna (HJ)

Ottendorfer, Oswald (HJ)

Otterburg, M. (K)

Otting, Rev. Prof. Bernard J. (R)

Otting, Rev. Prof. Henry W. (R)

Otto, August (H)

Otto, Carl (R)

Otto, Josef (H)

Ousterhaut, Cornelius (R)

Overholser, J. (R)

Overmeyer, Calvin Jennings (R)

Overrocker, Adam (R)

Pabst, F. (T)

Pabst, Fred (HJ)

Pabst, Fred Jr. (HJ)

Pabst, Fred C. (T)

Pabst, Friedrich (HJ)

Pabst, Gustav G. (T)

Padberg, John B. (R)

Paepke, Elizabeth (H)

Paepke, Hermann (H)

Paepke, Walter (H)

Paeschke, C. A. (T)

Pagenstecher, Felix (R)

Pahlmann, John (H)

Palme, C.J. (HJ)

Pangborn, William (R)

Pankow, A. (HJ)

Pankow, Pastor E.A. (GM)

Pantke, E. R. (T)

Papendieck, -- (K)

Papendieck, C. H. H. (HJ, K)

Papendieck, G. (HJ, K)

Parr, Philip (R)

Pasch, John (W)

Paschen, Geo. (HJ)

Pastorius, Franz Daniel (G2, R)

Patten, Phil. v. (HJ)

Pattengill, ALbert H. (R)

Patz, Adam (A)

Patz, Adam (A)

Patz, Amalia (A)

Patz, Augusta (A)

Patz, Augusta (A)

Patz, Bertha (A)

Patz (?), Bertha (A)

Patz, Gustav (A)

Patz, Herman (A)

Patz, John (A)

Patz, John C. (A)

Patz, Louise (A)

Patz, Michael (A)

Paul, Frank (W)

Paul, Martin (W)

Pauli, Henry Carl (R)

Pauling, William (R)

Paulsen, P. (HJ)

Paulus, Christ. (HJ)

Paulus, Francis Petrus (R)

Paulus, G. (HJ)

Paustian, Pastor, J.H. (GM)

Pavy, M. E. (H)

Payenstadt, Adolph (H)

Pechtold, Michael (W)

Peetz, Mathias (W)

Peighthal, George (R)

Pell, Captain John H. (G2)

Peller, Kunigunda (SH)

Peller, John (SH)

Pelosi, -- (HJ)

Pelot, Anna (A)

Pelot, Frederick (A)

Pelot, Gottlieb (A)

Pelot, Gustav (A)

Pelot, Regina (A)

Pelot, Wilhelm (A)

Peltzer, Otto (H)

Pelz, Henry (R)

Penner, Dr. L. (HJ)

Penschorn, Carl (T)

Pentillon, Dr. -- (K)

Perczel, Oberst Nicklaus (E)

Pereles, J. M. (HJ, T)

Pereles, Nathan (HJ)

Pereles, T. J. (HJ, T)

Periolat, Clemems (H)

Periolat, Veronika (H)

Perpich, Governor Rudy (G2)

Perrior, William (H)

Perrot, Nicholas (HJ)

Peschong, -- (HJ)

Peteler, Captain Francis (G2)

Peter, Georg (HJ)

Peter, William (R)

Peterman, Albert Edward (R)

Peterman, Henry C. (SH)

Peterman, Philapina (SH)

Petermann, Georg (H)

Peters, -- (K)

Peters, Charles (R)

Peters, Hugo (H)

Petersen, Adolph (E)

Petersen, Charles (H)

Petersen, Gerhard (E)

Petersen, Hermann (H)

Petersen, J. H. A. (HJ)

Petersen, Mrs. William F. (H)

Petersen, William F. (H)

Peterson, Gustav (HJ)

Petrie, Philipp (H)

Petsch, Hubert (W)

Petsch, Mathias (W)

Petsch, Peter (W, R)

Petterman, Amaly (SH)

Petterman, William (SH)

Peuschel, -- (K)

Peuser, Caroline (SH)

Peuser, Catharine (SH)

Peuser, Frederick (SH)

Peuser, John (SH)

Peuser, William (SH)

Pfaender, Catherine (SH)

Pfaender, William (G1, G2)

Pfaender, William (SH)

Pfaff, John A. (R)

Pfaffle, William (H)

Pfalzer, David M. (TC)

Pfau, Charles G. (SH)

Pfeifer, Ida (K)

Pfeifer, John (W)

Pfeiff, Andreas (SH)

Pfeiff, Catharina (SH)

Pfeiffer, Alexander (HJ, TC)

Pfeiffer, Alexander (H)

Pfeiffer, Caspar (H)

Pfeiffer, F. G. (E)

Pfeiffer, Friedrich (S)

Pfeiffer, George (SH)

Pfeiffer, Jost (SH)

Pfeiffer, Mary (SH)

Pfeil, Christian (HJ)

Pfeil, G. (K)

Pfeil, R. (K)

Pfeil, Rud. (T)

Pfister, Chas. F. (HJ, T)

Pfister, Elisabeth (HJ)

Pfister, Guido (HJ, K, R)

Pfitzer, Caspar (SH)

Pfitzer, Ernestine (SH)

Pflaume, Karl (G2)

Pfund, Dr. -- (K)

Pfund, John (H)

Pheff, Michal (R)

Philipp, A. F. (HJ)

Philipp, Adolph (HJ)

Philipp, Christ. (HJ)

Phillips, Lorenz (W)

Phineas, Brother -- (R)

Pick, Geo. (T)

Piening, A. (HJ)

Pieper, Prof. Aug. (GM)

Pieper, Rev. Aug. (HJ)

Pieper, Carl (HJ)

Pieper, Pastor J. W. F. (GM)

Pierz, Father (G2)

Pierz, Francis Xavier (R)

Pietsch, C. G. (K)

Pietsch, Karl (H)

Pietsch, Robert (H)

Pilger, Gustav (T)

Pillath, Charles (A)

Pillath, Gottlieb (A)

Pillath, Michael (A)

Pinten, Rt. Rev. Joseph Gabriel (R)

Piper, B. (HJ)

Piper, J. (HJ)

Piper, Martin (HJ)

Pirmian, Brother -- (R)

Pister, Rev. Jacob (TC)

Pitizel, John H. (R)

Pitschner, Carl (E)

Pittelkow, C. (T)

Plagge, Christoph (H)

Plagge, Heinrich (TC)

Plagge, Wilhelm (H)

Plank, -- (R)

Plank, Johann (H)

Plankinton, Wm. (T)

Plath, Herman (SH)

Plath, Louisa (SH)

Plathe, G. H. (H)

Plathner, A. (HJ)

Platte, Alexander (HJ)

Platte, Anton (W)

Platte, Eberhard (W)

Platte, Franz (HJ)

Platte, Joseph (W)

Platte, Peter (W)

Plattenberg, Josephine Howard (R)

Plattner, Solomon (R)

Platz, F. (HJ)

Platz, G.G. (H)

Platz, Rud. (T)

Plautz, Hermann (H)

Pleiss, Aug. (T)

Pless, Louisa (SH)

Pless, William (SH)

Plessner, Michael C. (R)

Plettel, -- (R)

Plewka, Frozyna (A)

Pline/Plein, Nicholas (W)

Plocher, Pastor J. (GM)

Plonke, Caroline (A)

Plonke, Ottilia (A)

Pludderman, -- (R)

Plumer, H. F. (E)

Plumhoff, August (R)

Plunky, Olga (A)
Poebel, Arno (H)
Poehler, Henry (G1)
Pohl, John Peter (W)
Pohl, Nikolaus (W)
Pohl, Paul (H)
Polasek, Alvin (R)
Pommer, E. (T)
Ponsly, J. (HJ)
Ponsly, R. (HJ)
Poppe, Prof. Ewald (E)
Poppe, M. A. (E)
Poppek, Mary (A)
Popper, J. (H)
Popper, J. G. (K)
Poppert, Georg (HJ)
Poppert, Henry (HJ)
Pors, W. A. (HJ)
Porter, John Frederich (R)
Porth, G. W. (HJ)
Posner, August (R)
Post, H. G. (K)
Potter, J. F. (HJ)
Pottgieser, Nicolaus J. (G2)
Prahl, Carl (SH)
Prahl, Wilhelmina (SH)
Pratt, Carl (HJ)
Prentiz, --, General (HJ)
Presser, William (R)
Pretorius, Emil (HJ)
Prezlaff, Fred C. (T)
Preuss, Prof. Francis A. (R)
Preusser, Ad. (K)
Preusser, Christian (HJ, K)
Preusser, Friedrich (HJ, K)
Preusser, Gustav (HJ, T)
Preutzer, Christ. (HJ)
Priebe, Wm. (E)
Prieger, E. (HJ, K)
Priester, Wm. (T)
Prietz, -- (K)
Prignitz, Caroline (SH)
Prignitz, Christine (SH)
Printy von Buchan, John (R)
Prinz, F. (T)
Pritzkow, -- (K)
Pritzlaff, John (HJ, K)
Pritzlaff, Fred C. (HJ)
Probstfield, Randolph (G2)
Prochatzka, A. (HJ)
Prosser, Engins (R)
Pruessing, Ernst (H)

Prussia, Christian (R)

Prutzman, Abraham C. (R)

Publow, Henry Lantz (R)

Puchner, Rudolph (HJ)

Puck, Joachim (E)

Pulcher, Martin L. (R)

Puls, Dr. A. J. (HJ, T)

Puls, Dietrich (HJ)

Pulte, Anton (W, R)

Pung, John (W)

Pung, Michael (W)

Pung, Paul (W)

Pung, Peter (W)

Putthoff, William H. (R)

Quant, Jacob (R)

Quarles, --, Kapitän (HJ)

Quentin, Karl (HJ)

Quimby, --, Senator (HJ)

Quincy, August (SH)

Quincy, Maria (SH)

Quinius, Hermann F. (S)

Raab, Georg (HJ)

Raabe, Wilhelm (HJ)

Raber, John (H)

Raber, Philipp (H)

Rabish, Ella Murazs (A)

Radcke, W. (K)

Raddicke, -- (R)

Rademacher, -- (K)

Rademacher, Bernard (W)

Rademacher, Franz (W)

Rademacher, Rt. Rev. Henry Jos. (R)

Rademacher, Heinrich (W)

Rademacher, Louise (R)

Radenhorst, Jacob (R)

Radke, J. (HJ)

Raggatz, J.H. (H)

Ragowski, Amortha (A)

Rague, Louis von (S)

Rahn, Henry G. (T)

Rahn, Hermann Ulrich (S)

Rahn, Otto (R)

Rahr, W. (HJ)

Rainer, W. (HJ)

Rakowski, Augusta (A)

Rakowsky, Maria (A)

Rakowsky, Michael (A)

Rakowsky, Wilhelm (A)

Ramien, H. W. (T)

Ramte, Paul (R)

Rantze, Hermann (H)

Rapp, Wilhelm (H, TC)

Rasche, Friedrich (S)

Rascher, Hermann (H)

Raseman, Richard E. (R)

Raskopf, Jacob (H)

Rasmussen, Dr. Hans (T)

Raster, Herman (G2)

Raster, Hermann (H, HJ, TC)

Rattenauer, Jacob (R)

Rattermann, H. A. (HJ)

Rau, C. (K)

Rauch, F. (K)

Rauch, G. (K)

Rauch, Johann (H)

Rauschert, Pastor -- (R)

Rauen, William (H)

Rausch, G. (HJ, K)

Rauschenberger, John (HJ)

Rauschenberger, W. G. (HJ)

Rauterberg, F. (HJ)

Ravour, August, Rev. (HJ)

Rebhan, Aug. (T)

Reck, Michael L. (G2)

Reckmeyer, Wm. (T)

Reding, N. (HJ)

Redmann, Henriette (SH)

Redmann, Michael (SH)

Reed, Pauline (H)

Reese, Hans (H)

Reese, Michael (H)

Regenfuß, F. (K)

Rehfeld, Angelie (SH)

Rehfeld, Frederick (SH)

Rehm, Dr. (K)

Rehm, Jacob (H)

Rehm, Johann (H)

Reich, David (H)

Reichart, August (R)

Reichel, H. J. (T)

Reichel, Louis (HJ)

Reichel, W. F. (T)

Reichenbach, Henry (R)

Reichert, Karl (H)

Reichert, William J. (TC)

Reid, William (R)

Reidenbach, Johannes A. (S)

Reidler, H. (R)

Reifschneider, -- (R)

Reighard, Jacob E. (R)

Reigle, David (R)

Reigle, Elias (R)

Reigle, John (R)

Reiker, George (R)

Reim, Prof. A. (GM)

Rein, Charles (R)

Rein, Emil (H)

Rein, Wilhelmina (R)

Reincking, C. D. (E)

Reinecke, Chas. (E)

Reineking, Friedrich (HJ)

Reiner, F. (H)

Reinhard, Dr. C. (T)

Reinhard, Catherine (SH)

Reinhard, Ignatz (SH)

Reinhard, Frau Louis (T)

Reinhard, Rob. (T)

Reinhardt, Henry (T)

Reinhardt, W. (K)

Reinhert, Walter August (R)

Reiniger, F. (K)

Reinsch, Prof. -- (HJ)

Reis, -- (K)

Reis, C. (K)

Reis, Peter (H)

Reis, Nicholas (H)

Reisenegger, Wilhelm (H)

Reitz, Charles (R)

Reitzel, Robert (R)

Rekow, Carl von (HJ, K)

Reller, Ernst (S)

Remeo, Paul (W)

Remien, William (H)

Rendtorff, Adolph (HJ)

Rendtorff, Edmund (HJ)

Rese, Rt. Rev. Frederick (R)

Rese, Friedrich (HJ)

Resofts, John (SH)

Reuben, Joseph (H)

Reuss, Fritz (T)

Reuss, G. A. (T)

Reuss, Gust. (T)

Reutel[s]hoefer, -- (HJ, K)

Reuter, Christoph (HJ)

Reuter, Prof. F.O. (GM)

Reuterdahl, Henry (H)

Reutschler, John (R)

Rheinhard, Louis (R)

Rhode, Caroline (A)

Rhorbur, Franz (HJ)

Rice, John (H)

Rice, J. H. (T)

Richard, Gabriel (HJ, R)

Richard, Heinrich (H)

Richard, Julius (HJ)

Richards, Daniel H. (HJ, K)

Richman, Charles H. (R)

Richter, Dr. A. (K)

Richter, Dr. A. J. (T)

Richter, Adolph H. (E)

Richter, Aug., Jr. (T)

Richter, Charles (H)

Richter, F. (HJ)

Richter, Gustav (HJ)

Richter, Rt. Rev. Henry Joseph (R)

Richter, Dr. Paul (E)

Richter, Theodore (R)

Rickenbacker, Eddie (H)

Rickenbacker, Edward V. (R)

Ricks, C.W. (HJ)

Ried, Henry (H)

Rieden, Frederick (R)

Rieden, Michael (R)

Riegel, Gustavus (R)

Rieger, Joseph A. (S)

Riehl, Ph. (K)

Riehl, Wilhelm Heinrich (G2)

Riem, R. L. (K)

Riemer, Gust. (HJ)

Ries, August (H)

Ries, Emil (H)

Ries, F. G. (HJ)

Riesdorf, Benjamin (R)

Riess, Johann J. (S)

Riess, Konrad (S)

Rietbrock, Adolph (HJ)

Rietz, Charles (H)

Rigge, Rev. Joseph F. (R)

Riggenbach, Johann Jakob (S)

Rinder, Friedrich (H)

Rindstopf, Sam. (HJ)

Rinehart, Thos. F. (R)

Rink, -- (K)

Rischatz, Dr. -- (K)

Rissenfeld, Catherine (SH)

Rissenfeld, John (SH)

Risthaus, -- (HJ)

Rittershaus, Emil (H)

Rittig, Jacob (TC)

Rittig, John (H)

Robbecke, Frederick (SH)

Robbecke, Herman (SH)

Robbecke, Sophia (SH)

Rockefeller, Johann Peter (R)

Rockey, John Wendel (W)

Rockstroh, John (SH)

Roddewig, F. (E)

Roden, Carl (H)

Roden, John (R)

Rodenbeck, W. H. (R)

Rodering, John (SH)

Rodering, Paulina (SH)

Rodermeyer, J. F. (H)

Roebbelen, Karl Augustus (R)

Röder, August (S)

Roeder, L. R. (HJ)

Roedder, Dr. E. C. (HJ)

Roehl, Wm. (SH)

Röhr, Julius (HJ)

Roehr, J. E. (T)

Röhrich, F. L. (T)

Roeline, Mina (SH)

Roemer, Prof. Charles (R)

Römer, G. (K)

Roemer, John (HJ)

Roemitz, C. F. (HJ)

Roeseler, John S. (HJ)

Roeseler, Karl (HJ)

Roeser, George (SH)

Roeser, Otto (R)

Roesing, Bernhard (H)

Roesser, William (R)

Rötzler, A. von Oels (K)

Rogers, C. C. (HJ)

Rogers, J. H. (HJ)

Rogge, Lorenz (E)

Rohlfing, Chas. (T)

Rohlfing, Wm. (HJ, T)

Rohlfing, Wm., Sr. (T)

Rohlfs, M. J. (E)

Rohmann, -- (HJ)

Rohnert, Morse (R)

Rohns, William C. (R)

Rohr, -- von, Hauptmann (HJ, K)

Rohr, Philip (G2)

Rohrbach, Heinrich (H)

Rolapp, Henry Herman (R)

Rolshausen, Ferdinand (H)

Rolshoven, Jules (R)

Roll, Francis (W)

Romanus, Christoph (H)

Romeicke, Herman (R)

Romes, Mathias (W)

Rominger, Dr. Carl Ludwig (R)

Ronge, Johannes (HJ)

Romanowsky, E. (S)

Rook, Peter (HJ)

Roos, Carl (SH)

Roos, Helene (SH)
Roos, Ernst (S)
Rosati, Bishop Joseph (TC)
Rosche, Chr. (HJ, K)
Rosche, J. (HJ)
Rose, Charles B. (R)
Rose, D. S. (HJ)
Rosebeck, J. (K)
Rosenbaum, Simon 9R)
Rosenberg, Hans (H)
Rosenberg, Jacob (H)
Rosencrantz, Clarissa (R)
Rosencrantz, Josiah (R)
Rosencrantz, Mortimer (R)
Rosenegk, A. N. (T)
Rosenfeld, -- (R)
Rosenfeld, M. (H)
Rosenstengel, W. H. (HJ)
Rosenthal, Dr. -- (K)
Rosenthal, --, Konsul (HJ)
Rosenthal, Hermann (H)
Rosenthal, Julius (H)
Rosenwald, Julius (H)
Rosenthal, Max (T)
Rosing, Anton Scheel (R)
Rosner, Charles (A)
Rosner, Christian (A)
Rosner, Louis (A)
Rosner, Louise (A)
Ross, George (SH)
Roß, W. (K)
Rossman, Stephen (R)
Rosswinkel, J. Rheinhardt (R)
Roth, Anthony (R)
Roth, Christian (R)
Roth, Filibert (R)
Roth, Frederick George (R)
Roth, J. (H)
Roth, J. R. (R)
Roth, William F. (R)
Roth, -- v. Eckstein (K)
Roth, Rev. Theodore (TC)
Rothenfeld, Heinrich (H)
Rothfels, Hans (H)
Rothmann, William (H)
Rothschild, A. M. (H)
Rothschild, Feist (R)
Rothschild, Kaufman (R)
Rothschild, Sigmund (R)
Rottmann, -- (K)
Rotz, --, General (HJ)
Rotz, August (HJ)

Rotzmann, P. (HJ)

Rowe, Lehrer [teacher] W. (GM)

Rubens, Harry (H, TC)

Rublein, George (R)

Rucker, Henry (H)

Rudhart, George Jacob (R)

Rudolph, -- (K)

Rudolph, Dr. A. A. (R)

Rudolph, Benjamin (R)

Rudolph, Joseph (H)

Rudzinski, T. (HJ)

Rueckheim, Mathilde (H)

Rügnitz, Chas. (E)

Ruehl, William (H)

Ruehle, Fred (R)

Ruehle, Godfrey Leonard Alvin (R)

Ruehle, John V. (R)

Rueping, Fred. (HJ)

Rüst, C. F. (HJ)

Ruete, I. W. (E)

Rütz, -- (K)

Ruffing, Augustine (R)

Ruhland, Hermann (H, HJ)

Ruland, Israel (R)

Ruland, William (R)

Rummel, E. (K)

Rumple, Herman (R)

Rundt, C. (K)

Runkle, George (R)

Rupp, Bernard H. (R)

Rupp, Peter (HJ)

Ruppe, Peter (R)

Ruppius, Otto (HJ)

Rusch, N. J. (E)

Ruschhaupty, G. (HJ)

Russ, Valentine (R)

Russer, Georg (H)

Sachs, Theodor (H)

Sack, -- (HJ)

Sälger, Anton (H)

Saenger, -- (HJ)

Saffert, Andreas (G2)

Sagendorph, Daniel P. (R)

Sager, Abram (R)

Saier, Felix Joseph (W)

Salamon, Bertha (T)

Salewski, Bertha (A)

Salewski, Fred (A)

Salewski, Frederick (A)

Salewski, Gustie (A)

Salewski, Ida (A)

Salewski, Ida (A)

Salewski, John (A)

Salewski (?), Louise (A)

Salewski, Martha (A)

Salewski, Michael (G2)

Salewsky, August (A)

Salewsky, Louise (A)

Salter, John (W)

Salter, John Casper (R)

Salomon, Chas. E. (HJ)

Salomon, Conrad (K)

Salomon, Eduard (HJ, K)

Salomon, Ernst (HJ, K)

Salomon, Friedrich (HJ)

Salsman, John G. (T)

Saltiel, Leopold (H)

Salzmann, Dr. Joseph (HJ, K)

Samuel, Christian (HJ)

Sanderl, Father Simon (R)

Sanders, Fred (R)

Sanders, Henry Arthur (R)

Sanders, J. (HJ)

Sanderson, E. (K)

Sanderson, Lilian (HJ)

Sanger, -- (K)

Sanger, Caspar M. (HJ)

Sanger, Joseph P. (R)

Sanne, Hertha (HJ)

Sanne, Frau Oscar (HJ)

Sateren, Martin Gerhard (R)

Sauber, Peter (R)

Sauber, W. F. (R)

Sauer, Rev. Christ (HJ)

Sauer, F. L. (K)

Sauer, Paul E. (HJ)

Sauer/Seuer, Peter Joseph (W)

Sauer, Wm. (HJ, K)

Sauer, Pastor Wm. (GM)

Sauerhering, Dr. (K)

Sauerhering, Edward (HJ)

Saupert, Albert (R)

Sauter, Charles (H)

Sauter, Jacob (H)

Sauter, Karl (TC)

Sauter, Vincent (H)

Schaack, Michael (H)

Schaaf, Anna Miss (R)

Schaaf, D. (K)

Schacht, William Henry (R)

Schacker, Rudolph (R)

Schade, Rev. M. (R)

Schade, Robert (HJ)

Schaeberle, John Martin (R)

Schaedler, Anna M. (TC)

Schaefer, Charles (R)

Schaefer, Frederick (H)

Schaefer, John L. (H)

Schaefer, Joseph (SH)

Schaefer, Leander (H)

Schäfer, Philipp (S)

Schaefer, Theresa (SH)

Schaeffer, A. H. (R)

Schaeffer, Rev. Bernard (TC)

Schaeffer, Dr. H. W. (HJ)

Schaeffer, Joseph (R)

Schafer, Anton (W)

Schafer, Anton (W)

Schafer, John (W)

Schafer, John Joseph (W)

Schafer, John Joseph (W)

Schafer, Mathias (W)

Schafer, Mathias (W)

Schafer, Michael (W)

Schafer, Michael (W)

Schafer, Michael (W)

Schafer, Peter (W)

Schafer, Theodore (W)

Schaffner, John Henry (R)

Schaffner, Joseph (H)

Schaffner, Louis (H, T)

Schafman, Rev. Henry A. (R)

Schairer, G. (H)

Schalch, F. A. (R)

Schall, Andreas (H)

Schaller, A. (H)

Schaller, Prof. J. (GM)

Schaller, Johann (H)

Schaller, Karl (S)

Schallock, W. (K)

Schank, Charles (R)

Schanck, L. G. (H)

Schandein, Emil (HJ)

Schandein, Emil, Jr. (T)

Schandlein, L. (T)

Schantz, --, Senator (HJ)

Schapekahn, Herman G. (G1)

Scharfenberg, H. G. (E)

Scharff, Gustav (HJ)

Schartuck, Walther (HJ)

Scharz, Peter (R)

Schauroth, Clemens (R)

Schebely, Jacob (HJ)

Schebosch, -- (R)

Scheele, Arnold (R)

Scheffer, Albert (G1)
Scheffer, Charles (G1)
Scheffler, Bernhard (SH)
Scheffler, Dorthea (SH)
Schefnicher, Joseph (R)
Scheibel, --, Professor (HJ)
Scheiber, Fred. (HJ, T)
Scheinpfing, F. (HJ)
Scheitel, Pastor Wilhelm (GM)
Schell, August (G1)
Schell, August (SH)
Schell, Theresa (SH)
Schelle, Fr. (S)
Schellenberger, Mary Etta (R)
Scheller, Dr. -- (K)
Schellhaus, Lorenz (R)
Schenck, Leopold (H)
Schenerman, Philip (R)
Schenk, Friedrich W. (S)
Schenkberg, -- (K)
Schenkendorf, Max von (G2)
Schenkoweitz, August (H)
Scherf, Pastor Paul (GM)
Scherff, J. (K)
Scherger, Georg (H)
Schermerhorn, -- (K)
Schermerhorn, John (H)
Schertel, Konrad (H)
Scherzer, Dr. (K)
Scherzer, Albert
Scherzer, Wilhelm (H)
Schesinger, Fred (T)
Schetky, Rev. George, D.D. (R)
Schetterly, George (R)
Scheuermann, Friedrich (H)
Scheutz, John C. (R)
Schevill, Ferdinand (H)
Schewe, August (A)
Scheyrz, Henry (R)
Schick, John (R)
Schickel, John (T)
Schiefflein, Jonathan (R)
Schierbaum, Johannes (S)
Schiessle, Georg (H)
Schifflein, Jacob (R)
Schill, Adolph (R)
Schillach, George Daniel (SH)
Schillach, Matilda (SH)
Schiller, Max (T)
Schilling, Adolph (SH)
Schilling, Barbara (SH)
Schilling, C. (H)

Schilling, Christine (SH)
Schilling, Frederick (R)
Schilling, Georg (H)
Schilling, George A. (TC)
Schilling, Louis (SH)
Schilling, Robt. (HJ)
Schimp, Peter (H)
Schimmelpfennig, Alexander (HJ)
Schindler, Abraham (HJ)
Schindler, Alwine (K)
Schindler, Balthasar (HJ)
Schindler, David (HJ)
Schindler, J. F. (HJ)
Schindler, Rudolf (H)
Schindler, Teresa (R)
Schinner, Aug. F. (HJ)
Schintz, Theodor (H)
Schippert, Dr. A. (K)
Schirmer, Friedrich (HJ)
Schirrmacher, H. (HJ, K)
Schivy, Carl (A)
Schivy, Charles (A)
Schivy, Frederick (A)
Schlach, Frederic Aigust (R)
Schlach, Leonard (R)
Schlacke, William E. (TC)
Schlacks, Heinrich (H)
Schlaeger, -- (TC)
Schlaeger, E. (H)
Schlapp, Aug. L. (E)
Schlatter, J. (K)
Schlatter, Michael (R)
Schlegel, Edward (TC)
Schlegelmilch, Christian (R)
Schleiermacher, Faithful (R)
Schleiermacher, Fried. (HJ)
Schleiger, J. (K)
Schleinitz, Emil von (HJ)
Schlenstedt, Fred. (HJ)
Schleret, Joseph (H)
Schlerf, John (HJ)
Schlesinger, -- (R)
Schlessinger, Ferdinand (R)
Schlicht, -- (K)
Schlicht, John Peter (W)
Schlichting, Amalie (H)
Schlichting, Amalie (SH)
Schlichting, Berthold (SH)
Schlichting, Ernst W. (HJ)
Schlichting, R. (K)
Schlick, Dorthea (SH)
Schlick, Lewis (SH)

Schlieter, --, Major (HJ)

Schlitz, John (HJ, K)

Schlitz, Joseph (HJ)

Schlitz, Victor (T)

Schloectmeyer, Prof. Hugo F. (R)

Schloemilch, Fr. (HJ, K)

Schloetzer, Georg (H)

Schloetzer, Rudolf (H)

Schloss, Emmanuel (R)

Schloss, Seligman (R)

Schlosser, Ensign (R)

Schlosser, J. H. (T)

Schlosser, Peter J. (R)

Schlueter, A. L. (T)

Schlueter, Hermann (HJ)

Schlundt, Johann Fr. (S)

Schmahl, Julius (G1)

Schmedding, Jan (R)

Schmedtgen, W. H. (H)

Schmelz, R. (K)

Schmeman, Karl (R)

Schmid, Emanuel (R)

Schmid, Pastor Frederick (R)

Schmid, Mathias (HJ)

Schmid, Robert (H)

Schmidel, Ulrich (G2)

Schmidhofer, Martin (H)

Schmidt, Frln. [Ms.] -- (K)

Schmidt, Anne (SH)

Schmidt, Anton Joseph (R)

Schmidt, Barney (E)

Schmidt, C. K. (R)

Schmidt, Carl (SH)

Schmidt, Carl Eugene (R)

Schmidt, Conrad (R)

Schmidt, Dorthea (SH)

Schmidt, Erich (H)

Schmidt, Ernst (H, TC)

Schmidt, F. (K)

Schmidt, Florian (H)

Schmidt, Fred (TC)

Schmidt, Frederick (H)

Schmidt, G. (K)

Schmidt, Georg (H)

Schmidt, Geo. J. (HJ)

Schmidt, Henry (SH)

Schmidt, Herbert William (R)

Schmidt, Hugo (H)

Schmidt, Jacob (G2)

Schmidt, Johann (H)

Schmidt/Schmitt, John Joseph (W)

Schmidt, Julius (H)

Schmidt, Karl H. (HJ)
Schmidt, L. M. (H)
Schmidt, Louis E. (H)
Schmidt, Louis Ernest (R)
Schmidt, M. (K)
Schmidt, Moritz (H)
Schmidt, Otto (H)
Schmidt, Dr. Otto L.(TC)
Schmidt, Richard (H)
Schmidt, Rud. (T)
Schmidt, Thomas (R)
Schmidt, Traugott (R)
Schmidt, Walter K. (R)
Schmidt, Wilhelm (H)
Schmidt, Wm. O. (E)
Schmidt, Rev. Winfried (E)
Schmidtill, S. (K)
Schmidtner, L. A. (K)
Schmitt, -- (R)
Schmitt, Frederick (H)
Schmitt, John (W)
Schmitt, John Adam (W)
Schmitt/Smith, John Peter (W)
Schmitt/Smith, Mathias (W)
Schmitt/Smith, Michael (W)
Schmitt/Schmith, Nikolaus (W)
Schmitt/Smith, Peter Hubert (W)
Schmitt, Quirin (W)
Schmittdiel, John (R)
Schmittdiel, John S. (R)
Schmitz, Pastor -- (K)
Schmitz, A. (HJ)
Schmitz, Ad. J. (T)
Schmitz, Catherine (SH)
Schmitz, J. Herbert (T)
Schmitz, John M. (W)
Schmitz, Joseph (W)
Schmitz, Louis (SH)
Schmitz, Maria (SH)
Schmitz, Michael (H)
Schmitz, Peter (H)
Schmitz, Peter Joseph (SH)
Schmorrenberger, Jacob (R)
Schnable, -- (R)
Schnack, Peter (R)
Schnacker, Rudolph (R)
Schnaeble, Jacob (H)
Schnaubelt, Rudolph (H, TC)
Schneckenburger, Joseph (R)
Schneider, -- (R)
Schneider, Dr. Adalbert (HJ, T)
Schneider, Barbara (SH)

Schneider, Bernhard (HJ)

Schneider, Casper, Jr. (W)

Schneider, Emil (HJ)

Schneider, Frau Emil (T)

Schneider, Engelbert (W)

Schneider, Francis Lee (R)

Schneider, Frederick (R)

Schneider, Georg (H)

Schneider, George (TC)

Schneider, George (SH)

Schneider, J. (H)

Schneider, John (SH)

Schneider, Dr. Joseph (HJ, T)

Schneider, Matthias (R)

Schneider, Otto (H)

Schneitmann, L. (H)

Schnickel, -- (K)

Schnitzius, Mary (SH)

Schnitzius, Peter (SH)

Schnitzler, -- (K)

Schnoepfel, Jacob (H)

Schnoerr, Mathias (HJ)

Schnol, John (R)

Schober, F. A. (R)

Schoeffler, Moritz (HJ, K)

Schoellner, F. W. (HJ, K)

Schoelltopf, J.H. (HJ)

Schoenauer, Emil (HJ)

Schönberg, A. (HJ)

Schoenefeld, Henry (T)

Schoenemsgruber, John George (R)

Schoenfield, -- (R)

Schoenhofen, Peter (H)

Schönemann, Anna Elizabeth (G2)

Schönleber, Otto J. (T)

Schoenwald, F. (H)

Schoepel, -- (HJ)

Schöttle, Johann G. (S)

Scholl, John William (R)

Scholtz, Adolph (TC)

Scholz, Hermann (E)

Scholz, Ignatius (R)

Schomisch, Nicholas (W)

Schons, Paul (G2)

Schontz, Homer Leroy (R)

Schory, Albert (S)

Schott, Franz (R)

Schott, Frederick (H)

Schotterbeck, Julius O. (R)

Schrader, Pastor C. (GM)

Schraeder, Fred (R)

Schramm, J. S. (E)

Schranck, H. C. (T)

Schrauben, John (W)

Schreck, John (W)

Schrembs, Rt. Rev. Joseph (R)

Schremser, Emil (R)

Schrenk, Christian (S)

Schrenk, Martin (S)

Schrödel, Pastor A. (GM)

Schröck, M. (K)

Schröder, -- (K)

Schröder, C. (T)

Schroeder, Edward (R)

Schroeder, Ernest (G2)

Schröder, Franz N. (E)

Schröder, Friedrich (E)

Schroeder, George (R)

Schroeder, Henry (G2)

Schröder, Henry II (T)

Schröder, J. N. (G2)

Schröder, James (E)

Schroeder, John (HJ)

Schröder, Lehrer [teacher] W. J. (GM)

Schroeder, W. (HJ)

Schroeter, August E. (HJ)

Schroeter, E. (K)

Schubert, Ernst (HJ)

Schubert, George P. (R)

Schuchardt, Louis (T)

Schuchner, A. (K)

Schucht, Emil (T)

Schuck, Henry (H)

Schuckmann, Charles (HJ)

Schuckmann, Frau C. (T)

Schueler, A. (HJ)

Schueller, Andrew (W)

Schueller, John (W)

Schueller, John Joseph (W)

Schünemann, Wilhelm (S)

Schüngel, P. (K)

Schürmer, Pastor Michael (GM)

Schuettler, Hermann (H)

Schuettler, Peter (H)

Schuetz, Fritz (HJ)

Schuetz, Johann Adam (R)

Schütze, Pastor M. (GM)

Schütze, Martin (H)

Schulde, Henry (SH)

Schulde, Matilda (SH)

Schulenberg, Charles (R)

Schuler, -- (K)

Schuler, A. D. (HJ)

Schull, Aaron G. (R)

Schull, Charles A. (R)

Schulte, B. (K)

Schulte, Casper (R)

Schulte, Joseph (H)

Schultz, Christian (SH)

Schultz, E. (K)

Schultz, Eduard (HJ)

Schultz, John R. (HJ)

Schultz, Katie (H)

Schultz, Lisette (SH)

Schultz, Louis F. (R)

Schultz, Nicolaus (H)

Schultz, O. (K)

Schultz, William F. (H)

Schulz, Charles (G2)

Schulz, Dan (K)

Schulz, J. H. (E)

Schulz, Joachim Fr. (S)

Schulz, Karl (G2)

Schulz, W. R. (HJ)

Schulze, Pastor K. F. (GM)

Schulze, Pastor W. J. (GM)

Schultz, H. F. (T)

Schumacher, -- (R)

Schumacher, Carl (SH)

Schumacher, E. (K)

Schumacher, F. (K)

Schumacher, Fred. (HJ)

Schumacher, John (W)

Schumacher, John (SH)

Schumacher, John Christian (SH)

Schumacher, Joseph (H)

Schumacher, Lina (H)

Schumacher, Louisa (SH)

Schumacher, Nicholas (R)

Schuman, Christophel (SH)

Schuman, Ephronzina (SH)

Schumann-Heink, Ernestine (H)

Schunck, Peter (R)

Schunk, -- (HJ)

Schurz, Carl (G1, G2, H, HJ, R, TC, T)

Schurz, --, Frau (HJ)

Schuster, J. B. (E)

Schuster, Wm. (HJ)

Schutt, Louis (H)

Schrup, N. J. (E)

Schwab, Charles (H)

Schwab, John Heinrich (R)

Schwab, Leopold (R)

Schwab, M. (K)

Schwab, Maria Elizabeth (W)

Schwab, Michael (H, TC)

Schwarthout, Antony (R)

Schwarting, H. (K)

Schwarting, H. H. (T)

Schwartz, Pastor -- (R)

Schwartz, B. S. (H)

Schwartz, C. W. (HJ)

Schwartz, Christian (HJ)

Schwartz, Fritz (HJ)

Schwartz, Heinrich (HJ)

Schwartz, J. E. (H)

Schwartz, Jerome B. (R)

Schwartz, John E. (R)

Schwartz, Philipp (HJ)

Schwartz, Rudolph (R)

Schwartz, William (R)

Schwarz, John (HJ)

Schwebach, --, Bischof (HJ)

Schwefel, H. (K)

Schweiker, Paul (H)

Schweitzer, Jos. (T)

Schwerdtfeger, August (SH)

Schwind, Dr. Peter (E)

Schwittay, Albert E. (A)

Schwittay, Caroline (A)

Schwittay, Elizabeth (A)

Schwittay, Frederick (A)

Schwittay, Gertrude (A)

Schwittay, Gottlieb (A)

Schwittay, Gustie (A)

Schwittay, John (A)

Schwittay, Samuel (A)

Schwittay, Samuel (A)

Schwittay, Theodore (A)

Sebring, Rudolph (R)

Seckinger, Bartholomew (W)

Seckinger, Fidel (W)

Sederick, John (R)

See, Gottfried (R)

Seebach, Marie (H)

Seebaum, J. A. (H)

Seeberger, J. D. (E)

Seebohm, H.A. (H)

Seeburger, R. (E)

Seefeldt, Meta (A)

Seefreid, -- (R)

Seeger, Eugen (H)

Seeger, J. (K)

Seeger, William (G1)

Seegmiller, William A. (R)

Seek, Conrad (R)

Seelenfreund, A. B..(TC)

Seeler, Hans (HJ)

Seelhorst, Justus (HJ)

Seelig, -- (R)

Seemann, E. (K)

Seemann, J. P. (HJ)

Segnitz, Ad. (T)

Sehlen, John C.H. von (HJ)

Seib, Christian (R)

Seibel, Georg (H)

Seibert, Dr. -- (K)

Seibert, J. A. (E)

Seibert, J. H. (E)

Seideff, -- (R)

Seidemann, Conrad (H)

Seidenburg, Frederick (H)

Seidensticker, Oswald (HJ)

Seider, August (SH)

Seider, Ida (SH)

Seidler, August (H)

Seidler, Ferdinand (H)

Seifer, Moritz (H)

Seifert, -- (K)

Seifert, Catherine (SH)

Seifert, Pastor Friedrich (GM)

Seifert, H. (K)

Seifert, Henry S., Jr. (T)

Seifert, John (SH)

Seifert, Rudolph (TC)

Seiffert, Rev. F. A. (R)

Seiman, Henry (R)

Seinholtz/Synold,
Dr. Carl Friedrich (W)

Seipp, Conrad (H)

Seipp, Mrs. Conrad (H)

Seipp, W.C. (H)

Seiter, Adolph (SH)

Seiter, Helena (SH)

Seitz, Fred (R)

Seitz, George (R)

Seitz, John H. (R)

Selig, William (H)

Seliger, William (H, TC)

Seligman, Jacob (R)

Seligmann, H. J. (T)

Selke, Esther (G2)

Selkrig, Rev. James (R)

Selle, August (H, TC)

Sellings, -- (R)

Selz, Lehrer [teacher] W. (GM)

Selzer, Rudolph (E)

Semmons, Cornelius (R)

Semrau, Pauline (A)

Semrow, Henry (H)

Sengstacke, John (H)

Senn, Nicholas (H)

Senner, Dr. -- (HJ)

Senninger, Nicholas (R)

Senter, M. D. (R)

Sentzke, Clara (SH)

Sentzke, Leopold (SH)

Serr, Conrad (SH)

Serr, Gabriel (SH)

Servatius/Servas, John Peter (W)

Seuel, Rev. C. (HJ)

Seybold, Johann (S)

Seyffardt, Ernst Julius (F)

Seyffardt, Ludwig (F)

Seyffardt, William (R)

Seyffardt, Wilhelm (F)

Shaeffer, Christian (SH)

Shaeffer, Henriette (SH)

Shaler, Heinrich (R)

Shape, C. T. (T)

Shape, Frau G. H. (T)

Sheavey (?), Anne (A)

Sheavey, Louis (A)

Sheman, Gustie (A)

Sherer, Amalia (SH)

Sherer, Peter (SH)

Sheteck, Augusta (A)

Shetteck (?), Louise (A)

Shetteck, Martha (A)

Shetteck, Michael (A)

Shevey, Carl (A)

Shevy, Augusta (A)

Shevy, Bertha (A)

Shevy, Caroline (A)

Shevy, Catherine (A)

Shevy, Charlotte (A)

Shevy (?), Charlotte (A)

Shevy, Fredericka (A)

Shevy, Frieda (A)

Shevy, Gustav (A)

Shevy, Gustav (A)

Shevy, Jennie (A)

Shevy, Julia (A)

Shevy, Lottie (A)

Shevy, Louis (A)

Shevy, Louisa (A)

Shevy, Louise (A)

Shevy, Louise (A)

Shevy, Martha (A)

Shevy, Mary (A)

Shevy, Mathilda (A)

Shevy, Michael (A)

Shevy, Michael (A)

Shevy, Michael (A)
Shevy, Michael (A)
Shevy, Minnie (A)
Shevy, Minnie (A)
Shevy, Regina (A)
Shevy, Seferin (A)
Shevy, William (A)
Shilling, Adolph (SH)
Shilling, Louise (SH)
Shimberg, Lillian Ruth (R)
Shivy, John (A)
Shoemaker, Michael (R)
Shoemaker, Robert (R)
Showalter, Conrad (R)
Shuman, Andrew (H)
Siebel, August (H)
Siebel, J.E. (H)
Siebel, Johann (H)
Sieben, G. (K)
Sieben, H. (K)
Sieben, Michael (H)
Siebenbrunner, Catherina (SH)
Siebenbrunner, Mathias (SH)
Siebert, Jacob (R)
Siebring, Adam (R)
Siegel, Franz (G1)
Siegert, John (T)
Siegler, Pastor J.C. (GM)
Siekmann, Heinrich (S)
Sievers, Ferdinand (G2, R)
Sigel, Franz (H, HJ)
Sigel, Hermann (HJ)
Silberzahn, -- (HJ)
Siller, Frank (HJ)
Silvestro, Clement (H)
Simon, -- (K)
Simon, Burghard (W)
Simon, Carl (SH)
Simon, David (SH)
Simon, F. (K)
Simon, H. (K)
Simon, John (H)
Simon, John Solomon (R)
Simon, Mathias (W)
Simon, Nic. (T)
Simon, Peter (W)
Simon, Philip (R)
Simon, Sigmund (R)
Simon, Sigmund (R)
Simonder, Carl (SH)
Simonder, Louisa (SH)
Sindt, This (E)

Singer, Emil (R)
Singer, Frederick (H)
Singelinger, Frederick (R)
Skillbeck, Jacob (R)
Slinger, John (R)
Sloman, Adolph (R)
Sloman, Mark (R)
Smeck, Eliza (SH)
Smeck, Werner (SH)
Smelzer, Nicholas (R)
Smeltzer, Arnold (R)
Smith, A. A. (T)
Smith, A. D. (K)
Smith, Abram (HJ)
Smith, Alb. (K)
Smith, Charles (SH)
Smith, Frederica (SH)
Smith, Geo. (K)
Smith, Henry (R)
Smith, J. B. (HJ, K)
Smith, J. G. (K)
Smith, Jacob (R)
Smith, John (SH)
Smith, Margaret (SH)
Smith, W. (HJ)
Smith, W. A. (K)
Smulders, Rev. Egidius (R)
Sneider, Cresenzia (SH)
Sneider, Crescenzia (SH)
Snitgen/Schnutgen, Franz (W)
Snyder, G. W. (R)
Soehler, Carl (SH)
Soehler, Sabine (SH)
Sokey, Albert (R)
Soloman, Archibald (R)
Solomon, E. S. (H)
Solomons, Ezekiel (R)
Sommer, Carl (SH)
Sommer, Elizabeth (SH)
Sommers, Jacob, Sr. (R)
Sommers, P. J. (HJ)
Sonday/Sontag, William (W)
Sonne, Carl (H)
Sonnen, Anton (SH)
Sonnen, Barbara (SH)
Sonnen, Thomas (SH)
Sonnenthal, -- (HJ)
Sonneschein, Dr. S. H. (E)
Sonntag, Frln. [Ms.] -- (K)
Sonntag, --, Jr. (K)
Sonntag, William Louis (R)
Sopher, Caroline (A)

Sorhagen, -- (K)

Sorter, George (R)

Soubron, Otto (HJ)

Soyer, Carl (H)

Spaan, H. (K)

Spackman, John (R)

Spangenberg, C. (K)

Spangenberg, E. (K)

Spanggenburg, Bishop -- (R)

Speckhardt, Gottlieb (R)

Speer, Charles (H)

Speich, Michael F. (R)

Speicht, -- (R)

Spelbrink, Christian (SH)

Spelbrink, Louise (SH)

Spell, Rudolph (R)

Spenkenberl, Rachel (R)

Spenner, John (SH)

Sperling, Ida (GM)

Sperling, Prof. J. E. (GM)

Spics, Aug. (HJ)

Spier, Frederick (R)

Spies, August (H, R, TC)

Spies, Augustus (R)

Spitzley, Henry (R)

Spitzley, John Jacob (W)

Spörl, J. (K)

Spoerni, John (HJ)

Spohr, Franz (H)

Spohrer, K. (H)

Spoor, A. (H)

Spranger, Francis Xavier (R)

Sprann, Henry (R)

Sprenger, Maria (SH)

Sprenger, Peter (SH)

Sprenger, Wentzel (SH)

Spring, G. (H)

Sprinkmann, Christ. (HJ)

Sprinkmann, Fred (T)

Stabell, Mathias (W)

Stable, Fred (R)

Stadler, Dr. -- (K)

Stadler, Anton (R)

Stahl, August (R)

Stahl, Jacob (R)

Stahl Joseph (R)

Stallo, -- (HJ)

Stamm, -- (K)

Stamm, Johann (HJ)

Stammler, George Frankeier (R)

Standau, Julius (H)

Stanger, Christoph (H)

Stanger, Daniel (H)

Stanger, Johann Georg (S)

Stank, Bertha (A)

Stank, Charlotte (A)

Stank, John (A)

Stank, Frederick (A)

Stank, Frederick (A)

Stank, Gottlieb (A)

Stank, Michael (A)

Stank, Minnie (A)

Stank, Mollie (A)

Stank, Samuel (A)

Stank, William (A)

Stankevitz, Adam (A)

Stankevitz, Mathias (A)

Stankevitz, Mollie (A)

Stankevitz (?), Wilhelmina (A)

Stannis, H. (HJ, K)

Stansing, Chas. (SH)

Stark, Christian (SH)

Stark, H. J. (T)

Stark, Maria C. (SH)

Stark, CHristoph F. (S)

Stark, Hy. J. (HJ)

Stark, Joshua (T)

Stark, Josua (HJ, K)

Starke, August (HJ)

Starke, Christoph (HJ)

Starke, Friedrich (HJ)

Starke, Henry (HJ)

Starke, Wilhelm (HJ)

Starker, C. H. W. (E)

Starks, A. W> (K)

Starzinger, Frank (E)

Starzl, John (E)

Staub, Rev. Clemens (G2)

Stauber, Frank A. (H, TC)

Stauber, Jacob (R)

Stauch, George Jacob (R)

Stauffacher, Anton (HJ)

Stauffacher, Henry (HJ)

Stauffacher, Jacob (HJ)

Stauffacher, Peter (HJ)

Stauffacher, Rudolph (HJ)

Steberle, Jacob (SH)

Steberle, Mina (SH)

Steche, -- (K)

Steck, Catherine (R)

Steck, George (R)

Steck, John (TC)

Steck, John (SH)

Steckel, Adrian (HJ, T)

Steeger, Edward (R)

Steffen, Aug., Sr. (E)

Stegemann, Gustav (E)

Steffens, Albert (R)

Steidle, Martin (H)

Steiger, Andrew (R)

Steimle, Adolph (SH)

Steimle, Wilhelmina (SH)

Stein, Carl (R)

Stein, Karl (R)

Stein, Karl (H)

Stein, Mathias (HJ, K)

Steinback, John (R)

Steinbeis, -- (K)

Steinbrook, Samuel (R)

Steindel, Bruno (H)

Steiner, Johann M. (S)

Steiner, Sergeant -- (R)

Steinert, Dr. Gottlieb (S)

Steinhauser, Philip (R)

Steinhauser, Henry (SH)

Steinhauser, Margaret[ha] (SH)

Steinhilber, Ezekiel (E)

Steinitz, Franz (H)

Steinlein, August (HJ)

Steinmann, -- (K)

Steinmann, H. J. (T)

Steinmann, John (HJ)

Steinmetz, -- (R)

Steinmeyer, -- (K)

Steinmeyer, Frau Wm. (T)

Steinwehr, -- (HJ)

Steinwyl, -- van (K)

Steppig/Steppich, Jacob (W) (W)

Stern, A. F. (T)

Stern, Bernhard (T)

Stern, Chas. G. (T)

Stern, Solomon (R)

Stern, Walter (T)

Stern, H. (HJ, K)

Stern, Herm. (T)

Stern, Henry (T)

Stern, Leo (HJ, T)

Sterneck, alias Adolph Scholtz (TC)

Sternlein, Andrew (SH)

Steuben, Baron -- (R)

Steyman, August (SH)

Stichler, George (R)

Stietz, O. (K)

Stintz, Otto (HJ)

Stirn, A. (T)

Stirn, August (HJ)

Stirn, H. (K)

Stirn, Henry J. (T)

Stirn, Marie (HJ, K)

Stempel, August (H)

Sten, Anton (H)

Stephan, Martin (H)

Stern, Max (H)

Stever, Edgar Z. (TC)

Stock, Frederick A. (H, TC)

Stoepel, William (R)

Störger, -- (K)

Stoetzel, John (H)

Stofer, J. (H)

Stohlmann, -- (K)

Stoll, Florentine (SH)

Stoll, Florence Amalia (R)

Stoll, Jacob (SH)

Stolze, -- (K)

Stolze, F. (K)

Stose, Clemens (H, TC)

Sträter, Kaspar H. (S)

Strakosch, -- (K)

Strang, Gabriel (R)

Strang, James L. (R)

Strasser, Jacob (E)

Straten, Hubert (H)

Straus, Leo (H)

Strauss, Richard (H)

Straussel, Martin (H)

Streeter, Adolphus (SH)

Streeter, Charlotte (SH)

Streicher, J. A. (H)

Streiff, Fridolin (HJ)

Streissguth, Otto (T)

Streit, John (R)

Streit, Karl F. (S)

Streitzguth, William (HJ)

Strelow, Albert (R)

Stresau, F. W. (T)

Stricker, David (R)

Stricker, Daniel (R)

Strippelmann, W. (H)

Strobel, A. (K)

Stroh, Julius (R)

Strohmann, Robert (HJ)

Strohmeyer, -- (HJ, K)

Strohmeyer, Chas. H. (T)

Strohmeyer, Geo. W. (T)

Strohmeyer, John F. (T)

Strothmann, Wilhelm (HJ)

Strohwaer, John (R)

Stronach, Joseph (R)

Struber, Ludwig (R)

Strubler, Georg (H)

Strüde, A. (K)

Struve, Otto (H)

Stubbs, Michael (R)

Stuch, J. F. (R)

Studer, Major A.G. (E)

Stuenkel, Friedrich (H)

Stütze, -- (K)

Stulle, Andreas (R)

Stumb, -- (K)

Stump/Stumpf, John William W)

Stumpenhausen, Henry (R)

Stupinski, W. (K)

Sturm, Bernhard (SH)

Sturm, Dorthea (SH)

Sturm, John (SH)

Sturm, Magdalena (SH)

Sturm, John Peter (W)

Sturm, Peter (W)

Stutte, A. (R)

Subilia, Augusta (SH) (SH)

Suchy, Rev. Leo (HJ)

Suder, Henry (H)

Suelflohn, A. F. (HJ, K)

Suhm, John J. (T)

Suhm, R. (HJ)

Suksdorf, C.L. (E)

Sulzer, A. (K)

Sulzer, Konrad (H)

Sulzer, T. C. (HJ)

Sunderlage, Johann (H)

Suppen, Solomon (R)

Suppus, H. (K)

Suther, H. (H)

Sutter, Brother -- (R)

Swaboda, Thomas (T)

Swartz, Deibert (R)

Sweitzer, Martin (R)

Sweitzer, Robert (H, TC)

Swensberg, Conrad G. (R)

Swenty, Augusta (A)

Swenty, Frederick (A)

Swenty, Jeanette (A)

Swenty, Louise (A)

Swenty, Mollie (A)

Swenty, Wilhelmina (A)

Swenty, William (A)

Suchalla, Anorta (A)

Suchalla, Frederick (A)

Syke, Peter (R)

Tachick, Charles (A)

Tachick, Charlotte (A)

Tachick, Emily (A)

Tachick, Frederick (A)

Tachick, Gusta (A)

Tachick, Gusta (A)

Tachick, John (A)

Tachick, John (A)

Tachick, Mollie (A)

Tachick, William (A)

Täuscher, -- (K)

Tams, Claus (HJ)

Tappek, Maria (A)

Tegge, C. E. (T)

Teichmann, William (H)

Teitel, Abraham (H)

Teller, E. E. (HJ)

Tenwinkle, Henry (R)

Tenzler, J. (K)

Tenzler, L. (K)

Terborg, Rev. J. E. (HJ)

Terchner, -- (R)

Terhorst, Gerhardt (R)

Tesch, J. H. (HJ, K)

Teschan, Dr. Rud. C. (T)

Teschemacher, -- (K)

Teschner, K. (H)

Tessmann, Karl (H)

Theil/Thiel, Christopher (W)

Theil/Thiel, John (W)

Theis, Karl (W)

Thelen, John (W)

Thelen, John Joseph (W)

Thelen, John Mathias (W)

Thelen, Mathias (W)

Thelen, Michael (W)

Theobald, Anna (SH)

Theobald, Louis (SH)

Theodor, -- (K)

Theurer, F. J. (T)

Theut/Theid, Jacob (W)

Thiele, Fr. (SH)

Thiele, William (SH)

Thiele, William, Jr. (SH)

Thielemann, Christian (H)

Thielmann, CHristian (TC)

Thien, H. (K)

Thierbach, A. (K)

Thierbach, Emilie (K)

Thies, Wilbur Herman (R)

Tholser, A. (H)

Thoma/Thome, Ulrich (W)

Thoman, Frederick (R)

Thomas, Calvin (R)

Thomas, Maggie (A)

Thomas, Theodor (H, TC)

Thome, Michael (W)

Thomen, Michael (W)

Thormaehlen, Anton (HJ)

Thuener, Heinrich (R)

Thuering, George (T)

Thuernau, Friedrich (H)

Thurmann, Carl (E)

Thurow, Pastor Th. (GM)

Thurtell, Henry (R)

Tibusch, Augusta (A)

Tibusch, Jennie (A)

Tiedemann, Nickolaus (E)

Tietsort, August (R)

Tillich, Paul (H)

Tillmann, John (W)

Tillmann, William (W)

Tilsner, Dr. H. L. (T)

Timbrink, John (HJ)

Timken, Henry (R)

Timme, Wilhelm (HJ)

Timpe, Aug. (E)

Tines, Henry (SH)

Tisch, Wm. (HJ)

Tisen, -- (R)

Toberer, John C. (SH)

Tölke, Heinrich (S)

Töpfer, P. G. (T)

Toll, Isaac De Graff (R)

Tomcek, Anna (A)

Toser, Herm. (T)

Träumer, Geo. B. (HJ)

Trapfer, Louis (HJ)

Traut, Jacob (R)

Trautman, Joseph (SH)

Trautmann, Philipp (H)

Trautwein, -- (K)

Trebra, -- von (HJ)

Tredupp, Chas. F. (HJ)

Treigehen, William (R)

Trenkamp, F. (K)

Trentlage, Georg (HJ)

Treusdell, E.W. (G2)

Trierweiler, Mathias (W)

Triesch, Irene (H)

Tripp, D. R. (HJ)

Tripp, Johannes (R)

Trischmann, Charles (HJ)

Tritschler, Philip (E)

Troeger, Georg (HJ)

Troester, John (R)

Trostel, A. O. (T)

Trostel, Albert (HJ)

Trostel, G. J. A. (T)

Troxler, Jacob (R)

Trumpff, G. E. (HJ)

Trustel, John (E)

Trzaska, Alexander (A)

Tschientschy, Fred (T)

Tschirgi, Mathias (E)

Tschudy, J.J. (HJ)

Tubefing, Fred (HJ)

Turner, Prof. F. W. (HJ)

Tuttas, Adolph (A)

Tuttas, Gust (A)

Twachtman, John (R)

Ubert, G. (K)

Ufer, Walter (H)

Uhl, Edwin (HJ, R)

Uhl, Henry (A)

Uhlensperger, J. (K)

Uhlich, -- (K)

Uihlein, Alfred (T)

Uihlein, August (HJ, T)

Uihlein, Chas. (T)

Uihlein, Edward G. (H)

Uihlein, Henry (HJ, T)

Uihlein, Wm. (T)

Ullrich, Louis (H)

Ullrich, M. (H)

Ulman, John (R)

Ulrich, Dr. -- (K)

Ulrich, Albert (H)

Ulrich, John (HJ)

Ulrich, John Peter (W)

Ulrich, Peter (R)

Ulrici, Emil (HJ)

Umbeck, Friedrich (S)

Umbeck, Friedrich A. (S)

Unger, Julius (H)

Unholtz, Catherine (A)

Unterherr, A. (H)

Unterkercher, George (R)

Upmann, D. (HJ)

Upmann, Hermann (HJ)

Upmeyer, W. H. (T)

Uppleger, -- (R)

Uthe, Christoph (H)

Vail, Levi (K)
Vajen, Carl (SH)
Vajen, Francisca (SH)
Vajen, Gottlieb (SH)
Vajen, Henry (SH)
Vajen, Maria (SH)
Valentiner, Dr. W. R. (R)
Van Armin John (R)
Van Dyke, John H. (HJ, T)
Van Erweyl, Arthur (HJ)
Van Glyck, -- (K)
Van Gresen (R)
Van Hise, Prof. -- (HJ)
Van Schaik, Isaac (HJ)
Van Staden, John (E)
Van Steenberg, Cecile (R)
Van Tyne, Claude H. (R)
Van Wagener, Ethel Philips (R)
Van de Vanter, Eugene (R)
Van de Walle, Jacob (R)
Vander Horck, Captain John (G2)
Vedder, Prof. Herman Klock (R)
Veers, -- (HJ)
Veit, -- (R)
Veith, A. G. (T)
Veith, Anton J. (HJ)
Venn, Dr. -- (K)
Vertin, Rt. Rev. John (R)
Vesenmeyer, Babara (SH)
Vesenmeyer, Ottilie (SH)
Vette, Wilhelm (HJ)
Vetter, Heinrich (G2)
Vianden, Harry (HJ, K)
Vianden, Heinrich (HJ)
Victorinus, Brother Imbert (R)
Vidior, Henry (R)
Vieau, J. (K)
Viehe, Kaspar H. (S)
Vilas, E. P. (T)
Vill, Kunigunda (SH)
Vill, Otto (SH)
Vilter, Wm. O. (T)
Viscoszky, Rev. Andrew (R)
Visqar, Jacobus (R)
Vliet, Garr. (K)
Vocke, Wilhelm (H, HJ, TC)
Vöchting, C. (T)
Völker, Anton (H)
Voelker, Paul Frederick (R)
Vogel, Dr. (HJ, K)
Vogel, August (HJ)
Vogel, A. H. (T)

Vogel, Barbara (SH)

Vogel, Fred. (HJ)

Vogel, Frederick, Jr. (HJ, T)

Vogel, Joseph (SH)

Vogel, Louise (HJ)

Vogel, Simon (SH)

Vogelgefang, F. (K)

Vogelsang, John ALbert (W)

Vognitz, W. (K)

Vogt, Henry (HJ)

Vogt, Johann (H)

Vogt, Joseph (R)

Vogt, William (R)

Voigt, -- (HJ, K)

Voigt, Anna (HJ)

Voigt, Carl G. A. (R)

Voigt, Edward W. (R)

Voigtlander, Walter (R)

Volckmann, Hugo (T)

Volk, Leonard (H)

Volkening, George L. (R)

Volmer,Anton (W)

Vollendorff, -- (HJ)

Vollert, Ed. (K)

Vollmer, Henry (E, H, TC)

Volz, Christian (R)

Volz, Emil Conrad (R)

Von Kocherthal, Joshua (R)

Von Kraut, Max (R)

Von Platen, Godfrey (R)

Von Reiswitz, Kurt, Baron von (TC)

Von Schelgel, Arthur (R)

Von Schon, Hans August Ewald Conrad (R)

Von Suchtelin, Franz Herman Hendrick (R)

Von Tungeln (R)

Vontobel, Jakob (S)

Voosen, Joseph P. (W)

Vosburg, Bernard (R)

Voss, Arno (H, TC)

Voss, Edward (H)

Voss, Ernest Carl Johannes (R)

Votz, Dr. Ernst (HJ)

Vrooman, Tunis (R)

Wachall, Martin (R)

Wacher, Charles (H)

Wachsmuth, Carl (E)

Wachsner, -- (TC)

Wachsner, Albert (H)

Wachsner, Leon (HJ, T)

Wack, Pastor Caspar (R)

Wacker, Charles H. (TC)

Wacker, Franz Joseph (W)

Wacker, Frederick (H, TC)

Wackler, W.F. (HJ)

Waechterhauser, Joseph (R)

Waechterhauser, Louis (R)

Wägli, S. (K)

Wagener, Jacob (SH)

Wagener, Max (R)

Wagener, William (R)

Wagner, --, Senator (HJ)

Wagner, -- (HJ)

Wagner, A. (K)

Wagner, Anna (R)

Wagner, August (SH)

Wagner, C. (K)

Wagner, C. H. (HJ)

Wagner, Carl (SH)

Wagner, Edward (R)

Wagner, F. (T)

Wagner, Frank Casper (R)

Wagner, H. C. (T)

Wagner, Hubert (HJ)

Wagner, J. (R)

Wagner, J. G. (HJ, T)

Wagner, John, Sr. (E)

Wagner, John A., Jr. (E)

Wagner, Julius G. (HJ)

Wagner, Karl (H)

Wagner, Dr. M. (K)

Wagner, Philipp (S)

Wagner, Ralph B. (R)

Wagner, William (H)

Wahl, Christian (H, HJ, T)

Wahl, Cornelius (W)

Wahl, Frederick (H, TC)

Wahl, Geo. H. (T)

Wahnke, John G. (SH)

Wahra, Ad. (T)

Wald, Adolph Nicholas (R)

Waldburger, -- (TC)

Waldeck, -- (K)

Waldeck, Jacob (T)

Waldmann, Heinrich (S)

Waldo, Jonathan (R)

Waldo, O. H. (K)

Waldorf, Frederick (R)

Waldseemüller, Martin (G2, R)

Wall, Edwin C. (HJ)

Wall, Georg Wendelin (S)

Wallber, Emil (HJ, T)

Waller, Anton (H)

Wallher, Albert (HJ)

Wallher, Emil (HJ)

Wallich, Adolph (HJ)

Waltensperger, Charles (R)

Walter/Waller, Francis (W)

Walter, Geo. H. (K)

Walter, Js. P. (K)

Walthausen, F. W. (R)

Walther, Arnold (H)

Walther, Dr. C. J. W. (HJ)

Walther, Dr. F. (K)

Walther, Georg (HJ)

Walthers, Ferdinand (TC)

Walzer, C. W. (E)

Wampler, Joseph (R)

Wanderlich, -- (HJ)

Wapler, A. G. (T)

Wappenhans, Charles Frederick (R)

Ward, Eber Brock (R)

Wardecke, Julius (A)

Wardner, Fr. (K)

Warncke, -- (HJ)

Warnecke, A. (HJ)

Warner, Hans B. (HJ)

Warner, Oscar (HJ)

Warthin, Alfred S. (R)

Wass, George (R)

Wasserman, Casimir (R)

Wassermann, Friedrich (H)

Watry, J.P. (HJ)

Watry, Ric. (HJ)

Watt, William Henry (R)

Waustinberg, Frederick (R)

Webber, Jacob (R)

Webber, W. A. (K)

Weber, Andrew (W)

Weber, C. B. (H)

Weber, Chr. (K)

Weber, Frederick (H)

Weber, Ellen (G2)

Weber, George (R)

Weber, Henry (T)

Weber, Henry (R)

Weber, J. (HJ)

Weber, J. A. (K)

Weber, John (H, HJ)

Weber, John, Sr. (E)

Weber, Joseph F. (R)

Weber, Mathias (W)

Weber, Theodor (H)

Weber, W. (K)

Weber, William C. (R)

Wechselberg, Jul. (HJ)
Weckler, John (H)
Wedemeyer, -- (HJ)
Wedemeyer, W. (K)
Wedemeyer, William W. (R)
Wedthoff, Albert (R)
Weeks, Dr. L. W. (K)
Wegener, -- (K)
Wegner, john (HJ)
Wehde, Albert (H, TC)
Wehe, -- (K)
Wehmhoff, Bernhard (HJ)
Wehmhoff, Eugen (HJ)
Wehmhoff, Heinrich (HJ)
Wehmhoff, Josephine (HJ)
Wehmhoff, Leo (HJ)
Wehner, Herman (R)
Wehner, Wilh. (HJ)
Wehr/Weher, Anthony (W)
Wehr, Henry (T)
Wehrs, Helena (SH)
Wehrs, Theodore (SH)
Weibrecht, Louis (HJ)
Weid, Alexander (H)
Weidner, Paul (R)
Weidzel, Jacob (H)
Weigand, -- (R)
Weigel, Julius (HJ)
Weigell, Aug. (T)
Weihbrecht, L. (K)
Weikamp, George B. (R)
Weil, Charles L. (R)
Weil, Benj. M. (T)
Weiland, Nikodamus (W)
Weimer, Albert Carl (R)
Weimer, George E. (R)
Weinberg, E. (K)
Weinebrodt, Oscar (H)
Weinem, Dr. (K)
Weinert, Adolph (H)
Weinert, Albert (R)
Weinhagen, Fred. (T)
Weinhagen, Geo. (T)
Weinmann, Pastor -- (K)
Weinman, Adolph Alexander (R)
Weinmann, Heinrich (H)
Weippiert, J. W. (E)
Weirich, Peter (R)
Weis, Gustav (E)
Weis, Carl (T)
Weisbrod, Wm. (E)
Weiskopf, Leopold (G2)

Weiskopf, Rosa (G2)
Weiss, Gerhard (G2)
Weiss, Gross (R)
Weiss, J. P. (R)
Weiss, John B. (TC)
Weiss, Sebastian (S)
Weissenborn, Rudolf (H)
Weissenhagen, John P. (R)
Weissensel, August (H)
Weissgerber, F. F> (S)
Weissmann, Henry (TC)
Weiß, Charles, Sr. (E)
Weiß, G. E. (HJ)
Weiße, Dr. -- (K)
Weiße, Amalie (K)
Weiße, Chas. S. (HJ)
Weißenborn (K)
Weißkirch, Emil (HJ)
Weißkirch, E. (K)
Weitbrecht, Gotthilf (S)
Weitling, -- (TC)
Weitzel, -- (HJ)
Weitzel, Col. Godfrey (R)
Weitzel, Jacob (W)
Weitzel, John (R)
Welb, Ferdinand (HJ, TC)
Welb, Fred (T)
Welb, Friedich (H)
Weld, Wm. F. (R)
Welde, Carl (R)
Weller, Ferdinand (R)
Weller, Frederick (R)
Weller, Joseph (R)
Wellmacher, John (H, TC)
Wellskopf, John (A)
Welsch, Johann P. (S)
Welte, Casper (W)
Weltz, Robert (R)
Welz, George (R)
Welz, Jacob (R)
Welz, Philip (R)
Welz, Dr. Walter (R)
Welz, Wilhelmina (R)
Wendel, Dr. W. C. (T)
Wendt, Chas. A. (T)
Wendt, Chas. E. (HJ, K)
Wendt, Mathilde (K)
Wendt, Henry (H)
Wendt, Wylie Brodbeck (R)
Wendte, R. (K)
Weng, Rev. G. (HJ)
Wengler, -- (K)

Weninger, Francis Xavier (R)
Wenninger, Pater -- (K)
Wenter, Frank (H)
Wenter, Frederick (H)
Wentz, Abdel (G2)
Wentz, Christian (H)
Wentz, E. L. (R)
Wentz, John (R)
Wenzlick, -- (K)
Werbke, Hermann (HJ)
Werdehoff, H. (HJ, K)
Wermers, Bernard J. (R)
Wernar, Kiester (R)
Werner, Wm. (HJ)
Wernich, G. (HJ)
Wertelewski, Gottlieb (A)
Wertelewski, John B. (A)
Wertelewski, Lydia (A)
Wertelewski, Wilhelmina (A)
Werthmüller, -- (E)
Wertmuller, -- (R)
Weschecke, Dr. Carl F. (SH)
Wesemann, Rev. F. (HJ)
Wesener, Hugo (R)
Wesenheft, Charles (TC)
Weskowski, Ludwig (R)
Wessling, Hermann (H)
West, -- (K)
Westerfeld, J.H. (H)
Westfall, -- (HJ)
Westkamp, Bernhard (H)
Westphal, August (SH)
Westphal, Florentine (SH)
Westrick, -- (R)
Wetten, Emil (H)
Wetterström, Pastor -- (K)
Wettle, Johann (S)
Wettstein, H. (K)
Wettstein, Theodor (HJ, K)
Wettstein, Th., Jr. (K)
Weydenmeyer, Joseph (TC)
Weyerhauser, Frederick (R)
Weyker, J. (HJ)
White, John A. (Bialy) (A)
White, Fred (A)
White, Frederick (A)
White, Jennie (A)
White, Michael (A)
White, Minnie (A)
Wicker, Charles (H)
Wichman, Dietrich (SH)
Wichman, Rebecca (SH)

Widl, F. S. (E)
Widule, Christ. (HJ)
Wieber, Conrad (W)
Wieber, Joseph (W)
Wieber, Ludwig (W)
Wieber, Peter (W)
Wieboldt, Mrs. W.A. (H)
Wiechmann, Pastor F. (GM)
Wiedinger, Karl (H)
Wiedman, John (SH)
Wiedman, Margaretta (SH)
Wielandt, -- (K)
Wiener, Alexander (H)
Wier, J.B. (H)
Wier, Wilhelm (G2)
Wier, Pastor Wilhelm (GM)
Wiesenkraft, Charles (H)
Wiesenkraft, William (H)
Wiesner, Eduard (HJ, K)
Wiest, G. F. (E)
Wiethoff, Wilhelm (R)
Wilczewski, Rev. Joseph (R)
Wild, C. E. (T)
Wild, Henry (HJ, K)
Wild, Hilarius (HJ)
Wilhelmi, Dr. -- (K)
Will, Adam (A)
Will, Carl (A)
Will, Jacob (A)
Will, Johannes (S)
Will, Louise (A)
Will, Michael (A)
Will, Philipp (H)
Will (?), Wilhelmina (A)
Willgohs, Dr. -- (K)
Willich, M. T. (K)
Willig, August (HJ)
Willius, Ferdinand (G2)
Willius, Fredrick (G2)
Willius, Gustav (G2)
Willmanns, A. C. (HJ, K)
Willmanns, Fr. (K)
Willmanns, Frau F. (T)
Willmarth, H. M. (TC)
Willner, E.G. (H)
Wilmers, John (H)
Wiltberger, Percy Barnet (R)
Winans, -- (HJ)
Winckler, Willibald (H)
Wind, -- (K)
Winkelman, Caroline (SH)
Winkelman, Julia (SH)

Winkelman, Wm. (SH)

Winkelman, William (SH)

Winkler, C. (K)

Winkler, Carl (HJ)

Winkler, Caroline (SH)

Winkler, F. (H)

Winkler, F. C. (HJ, K, T)

Winkler, Fred. C. (HJ)

Winkler, Henrietta (SH)

Winkler, Herman (SH)

Winkler, John Frederick (R)

Winkler, Max (R)

Winkle, -- (R)

Winter, Rev. -- (HJ)

Winter, Pastor A. F. (GM)

Winter, H. A., Rev. (HJ)

Winter, J. (K)

Winter, Michael (HJ)

Winterall, Felix (SH)

Winterfeld, Chas. (HJ)

Winterhalter, Albert Gustavus (R)

Winterhalter, Michael (R)

Wintermeyer, Gustav (HJ)

Wintermeyer, Valentin (HJ)

Winterstein, Hermansan [?] (R)

Wintner, Rabbi Dr. Leopole (G2)

Wipf, -- (HJ)

Wirt, David (R)

Wirth, Peter (W)

Wise, -- (K)

Wist, Casimer (H)

Witmer, Jacob (R)

Witner, Lorenz (R)

Wittgen, John (W)

Witte, -- (K)

Witte, Karl Fr. (S)

Wittenmeyer, John (R)

Wittig, L. (K)

Wittlock, Ernest (R)

Wittmann, -- (K)

Wittmann, Adolph (HJ)

Wittmann, Anna Christina (HJ)

Wode, John (H)

Woehrly, Rudolf (H)

Woelfel, Henry (H)

Wohlfert/Wohlfahrt, Franz Joseph (W)

Wohlgemuth, R. (E)

Wohlscheid, Nicholas (W)

Wohlscheid, Peter (W)

Wolf, -- (HJ)

Wolf, Adam (H)

Wolf, F. W. (H)

Wolf, Jacob (R)

Wolf, John (R)

Wolf, Josef (H)

Wolf, W. H. (HJ)

Wolff, -- (K)

Wolff, Albert (G1, G2)

Wolff, Ludwig (H)

Wolfinger, Thomas (H)

Wolfskeel, Karl von (H)

Wollaeger, Gustav (HJ, T)

Wolläger, Franz (HJ, T)

Wollenwebber, Mathias (R)

Wollmer, R. (HJ, K)

Woltersdorf, Arthur (H)

Wonderlich, Nicholas (R)

Worpenberg, George (R)

Wramplemeier, Theodore John (R)

Wrisberg, Alfred (HJ)

Würst, -- (K)

Würtz, H. E. (H)

Wuertzner, Joseph (R)

Wulff, Henry (H)

Wulfmann, C. Heinrich (S)

Wunder, Rev. Henry (TC)

Wunder, Heinrich (H)

Wunderly, -- (K)

Wunderly, Dr. (HJ, K)

Wundsch, Dr. (K)

Wunsch, Henry (R)

Wunsch, William Frederick (R)

Wurster, Alexander (H, TC)

Yahr, Eugene F. (T)

Yahr, Fred (T)

Yeiser, Engelhardt (R)

Youngerman, Conrad (E)

Youngerman, F. W. (E)

Yunck, Wilhelm (R)

Zabel, Paul (T)

Zägel, Joseph (H)

Zagray, Emily (A)

Zahn, H. H. (T)

Zaiser, Rev. Arthur (E)

Zalle, H. (H)

Zander, Henry (H)

Zander, Henry G. (TC)

Zander, L. T. (K)

Zander, M. J. (K)

Zander, S. B. (K)

Zanelius, John George (R)

Zapp, August (H)

Zapp, Edward A. (G2)

Zapp, Edward J. (G2)

Zastrow, B. von (T)

Zautke, H. (HJ)

Zedler, Prof. John (R)

Zedler, Otto A. (T)

Zedler, R. (K)

Zeigler, John C. (R)

Zeigler, Rev. Paul (R)

Zeimetz, Peter (W)

Zeininger, Monsignore (HJ)

Zeisberger, -- (R)

Zeisler, Ernst (H)

Zeisler, Samuel (TC)

Zeller, Albert (S)

Zenger, John Peter (R)

Zepter, G. J. (E)

Zermer, -- (R)

Zervas, Matthew (W)

Zettel, Barbara (SH)

Zettel, John (SH)

Zettler, Emil R. (H)

Zeug, Dorthea (SH)

Zeug, John (SH)

Zeug, Ursula (SH)

Zich, Präses [title] A.F. (GM)

Ziegfeld, Dr. -- (TC)

Ziegfeld, Florence (H)

Ziegfeld, Florenz (TC)

Ziegle, Christ (R)

Ziegler, Alexander (HJ)

Ziegler, August (SH)

Ziegler, August (SH)

Ziegler, Brauer -- (K)

Ziegler, Ed. (T)

Ziegler, Karl (H)

Ziehn, Bernhard (H)

Zielsdorf, Otto (T)

Ziller, John (HJ)

Zimbelmann, John (E)

Zimmer, Conrad (W)

Zimmerman, Eugene (R)

Zimmerman, John F. (R)

Zimmermann, A. G. (H)

Zimmermann, Adolph (HJ)

Zimmermann, Dr. C. (T)

Zimmermann, D. C. (H)

Zimmermann, Dr. E. (K)

Zimmermann, G. E. (H)

Zimmermann, Hans J. (H)

Zimmermann, H. W. (H)

Zimmermann, Johannes (S)

Zimmermann, John (W)

Zimmermann, Nicholaus (HJ)

Zinkeisen, H. (K)

Zinn, A. C. (T)

Zinn, Adolph (HJ)

Zinn, Albert (T)

Zins, John (HJ)

Zinzendorff, -- (R)

Zirndorff, Rabbi Heinrich (R)

Zitez, Mary (A)

Ziwet, Albert (R)

Zöhrlaut, Edward (HJ, T)

Zöhrlaut, Hermann (HJ, K)

Zoellner, Frank (R)

Zoliski, J. (H)

Zolly, Felix (R)

Zschwetsche, Theo. (HJ)

Zucker, Adolph Edward (R)

Zündt, Ernst Anton (HJ, K)

Zunderman, John (R)

Zwietusch, O. (K)

Zwolanek, Johannes (S)

Zysk, Tom (A)

## Other Works by The Editor

*German-Americana: A Bibliography*. Scarecrow Press, 1975.

*America's German Heritage*. German-American National Congress, 1976.

*German-American Literature*. Scarecrow Press, 1977.

*Festschrift for the German-American Tricentennial Jubilee: Cincinnati 1983*. Cincinnati Historical Society, 1982.

*The Cincinnati Germans after the Great War*. Peter Lang Pub. Co., 1987.

*The First Description of Cincinnati and Other Ohio Settlements: The Travel Report of Johann Heckewelder, 1792*. University Press of America, 1988.

*Spring Grove and Its Creator: H. A. Rattermann's Biography of Adolph Strauch*. Ohio Book Store, 1988.

*Catalog of the German-Americana Collection, University of Cincinnati*. K.G. Saur, 1990.

*The First Mayor of Cincinnati: George A Katzenberger's Biography of Major David Ziegler*. University Press of America, 1990.

*New German-American Studies*. Peter Lang Pub. Co., 1990- .

*Germany and America (1450-1700): Julius Friedrich Sache's History of the German Role in the Discovery, Exploration and Settlement of the New World*. Heritage Books, Inc., 1991.

*The First Germans in America, With a Biographical Directory of New York*. Heritage Books, Inc., 1992.

*In der Neuen Welt: Deutsch-Amerikanische Festschrift fuer die 500-Jahrfeier der Entdeckung von Amerika*. Peter Lang Pub. Co., 1992.

*Ohio Valley German Biographical Index*. Heritage Books, Inc., 1992.

*Ohio Valley German Biographical Index - A Supplement*. Heritage Books, Inc., forthcoming.

Heritage Books by Don Heinrich Tolzmann:

*Amana: William Rufus Perkins' and Barthinius L. Wick's History of the Amana Society, or Community of True Inspiration*

*Americana Germanica: Paul Ben Baginsky's Bibliography of German Works Relating to America, 1493–1800*

*Biography of Baron Von Steuben, the Army of the American Revolution and Its Organizer: Rudolf Cronau's Biography of Baron von Steuben*

*CD: German-American Biographical Index (Midwest Families)*

*CD: Germans, Volume 2*

*CD: The German Colonial Era (four volumes)*

*Cincinnati's German Heritage*

*Covington's German Heritage*

*Custer: Frederick Whittaker's Complete Life of General George A. Custer, Major General of Volunteers, Brevet Major General U.S. Army and Lieutenant-Colonel Seventh U.S. Cavalry*

*Dayton's German Heritage: Karl Karstaedt's Golden Jubilee History of the German Pioneer Society of Dayton, Ohio*

*Early German-American Newspapers: Daniel Miller's History*

*German Achievements in America: Rudolf Cronau's Survey History*

*German Americans in the Revolution*

*German Immigration to America: The First Wave*

*German Pioneer Life and Domestic Customs*

*German Pioneer Lifestyle*

*German Pioneers in Early California: Erwin G. Gudde's History*

*German-American Achievements: 400 Years of Contributions to America*

*German-Americana: A Bibliography*

*Germany and America, 1450–1700*

*Kentucky's German Pioneers: H. A. Rattermann's History*

*Lives and Exploits of the Daring Frank and Jesse James: Thaddeus Thorndike's Graphic and Realistic Description of Their Many Deeds of Unparalleled Daring in the Robbing of Banks and Railroad Trains*

*Louisiana's German Heritage: Louis Voss' Introductory History*

*Maryland's German Heritage: Daniel Wunderlich Nead's History*

*Memories of the Battle of New Ulm: Personal Accounts of the Sioux Uprising. L. A. Fritsche's History of Brown County, Minnesota (1916)*

*Michigan's German Heritage: John Andrew Russell's History of the German Influence in the Making of Michigan*

*Ohio's German Heritage*

*Outbreak and Massacre by the Dakota Indians in Minnesota in 1862: Marion P. Satterlee's Minute Account of the Outbreak, with Exact Locations, Names of All Victims, Prisoners at Camp Release, Refugees at Fort Ridgely, etc. Complete List of Indians Killed in Battle and Those Hung, and Those Pardoned at Rock Island, Iowa*

*The German Element in Virginia: Herrmann Schuricht's History*

*The German Immigrant in America*

*The Pennsylvania Germans: James Owen Knauss, Jr.'s Social History*

*The Pennsylvania Germans: Jesse Leonard Rosenberger's Sketch of Their History and Life*

*Upper Midwest German Biographical Index*

www.ingramcontent.com/pod-product-compliance
Lightning Source LLC
LaVergne TN
LVHW061248100826
845148LV00008B/1059